THE LANGUAGE *of* LOVE & RESPECT

WORKBOOK

DR. EMERSON EGGERICHS

THOMAS NELSON
Since 1798

NASHVILLE   DALLAS   MEXICO CITY   RIO DE JANEIRO   BEIJING

Published in Nashville, Tennessee, by Thomas Nelson. Thomas Nelson is a registered trademark of Thomas Nelson, Inc.

Thomas Nelson, Inc. titles may be purchased in bulk for educational, business, fund-raising, or sales promotional use. For information, please e-mail SpecialMarkets@ThomasNelson.com.

Emerson Eggerichs is represented by the literary agency of Alive Communications, Inc., 7680 Goddard Street, Suite 200, Colorado Springs, CO 80920. www.alivecom.com.

All Scripture quotations, unless otherwise indicated, are taken from the NEW AMERICAN STANDARD BIBLE® (NASB), © The Lockman Foundation 1960, 1962, 1963, 1968, 1971, 1972, 1973, 1975, 1977, 1995. Used by permission.

Additional Scripture quotations are taken from the following sources:
The King James Version (KJV). Public domain. *The Message* (MSG) by Eugene H. Peterson. © 1993, 1994, 1995, 1996, 2000. Used by permission of NavPress Publishing Group. All rights reserved. HOLY BIBLE: NEW INTERNATIONAL VERSION® (NIV®). © 1973, 1978, 1984 by International Bible Society. Used by permission of Zondervan. All rights reserved. The New International Reader's Version® (NIrV®). © 1996, 1998 International Bible Society. All rights reserved throughout the world. Used by permission of International Bible Society. *Holy Bible,* New Living Translation (NLT). © 1996. Used by permission of Tyndale House Publishers, Inc., Wheaton, Illinois 60189. All rights reserved. THE ENGLISH STANDARD VERSION (ESV). © 2001 by Crossway Bibles, a division of Good News Publishers. Used by permission. All rights reserved. Today's English Version (TEV), © American Bible Society 1966, 1971, 1976, 1992.

Interior Design: Rainbow Graphics, Kingsport, TN.

Previously released as *Cracking the Communication Code Workbook*, ISBN: 978-0-7852-2842-4

ISBN: 978-0-8499-4696-7

Printed in the United States of America
09 10 11 12 13 RRD 7 6 5 4 3 2 1

CONTENTS

BEFORE YOU BEGIN YOUR STUDY OF
The Language of Love & Respect . . .

Welcome to the *The Language of Love & Respect Workbook* experience! You are about to discover and apply a truth hidden in plain sight in the Bible for 2000 years! This secret can affect your marital communication in powerful ways. Today, you and your spouse can start new with the biblical truths on marital communication given in this workbook and the book it accompanies—*The Language of Love & Respect*. These two books serve as companions to help you crack the code to marital communication.

Based on three decades of counseling experience and scientific and biblical research, the book—*The Language of Love & Respect*—offers you the information and tools you will need to understand what is wrong in your communication and how to start correcting it. This workbook gives you and your mate a private place to finish a wide variety of exercises that help you apply these communication insights to your marriage.

Before you begin your study, consider these helpful hints as you attempt to change and enrich your marital communication:

Come ready to let God help you work on your marriage. As you experience *The Language of Love & Respect*, God intends to amaze you with His help. (Jesus calls the Holy Spirit the Helper!) As you open your heart to Him, you will discover His truth in Ephesians 5:33 guiding you to communicate in new and refreshing ways. This is no quick fix, but if you spend a reasonable amount of time and effort, and put into action the tiniest of changes, God will use this study in your life.

Study at your own pace, but keep studying. Some questions will strike you as simple—others take more thought and effort. As you interact with the concepts in *The Language of Love & Respect*, marital communication becomes "doable." Yes, it takes work but God never intended communication to be complex between husband and wife. Though misunderstandings happen in abundance, the love and respect method prevents you from nose-diving, crashing, and burning! So, keep studying. Don't quit when you or your spouse don't immediately "get it." See these as bumps in the road, not roadblocks. Keep studying! Also, do not try to cover every last question. Concentrate on the questions that speak to your needs as husband and wife.

Become familiar with how this workbook is constructed. It covers the *The Language of Love & Respect* book in twelve sessions. Some sessions cover only one chapter of the book; others cover more than one chapter. Get involved with the questions. Keep the big picture in mind as you try to apply love and respect to your communication in marriage. Note that a title heads each question to allow you to quickly identify the focus.

You can study this book solo but preferably as a couple. For greatest benefit, study with your spouse. Both of you should share your answers where appropriate. As you talk about your answers, you will gain new understanding of each other and this will improve communication. If your spouse shows disinterest in studying *The Language of Love & Respect*, you can gain much from working alone. As you start putting the communication principles into action, your spouse may decide to join you!

Treat each other with Love and Respect. Because some questions probe sensitive areas, tension will develop—even irritation and anger. The rule is: when dealing with sensitive issues, be sensitive to each other! If a question becomes a bit too sticky, and one of you doesn't feel up to dealing with it, table that question for discussion later.

Handle each other with care. As you continue the study, you will soon see that a question may show the strength of one spouse and the vulnerability of the other. Where you have natural strengths and knowledge, your spouse may feel vulnerable and inadequate. Always remember that God created us male and female—not wrong, just different. If you approach each question with compassion and empathy, the weaker will not feel judged by the stronger. Consequently, the vulnerable one will feel a greater freedom to deal with the topic and get feelings on the table.

As you study, realize God is drawing you to Himself, so keep praying! *The Language of Love & Respect* puts you in closer touch with your spouse, but the ultimate goal is to put you in closer touch with your Lord. Every session in this workbook rests on God's revelation to you in Ephesians 5:33. So, pray that the Lord keeps revealing His will about applying love and respect to your mouth! Without prayer, as a follower of Christ, your study will yield few returns. Pray without ceasing, and you will see God work at His pace, in His way, as He strengthens you "with power through His Spirit in the inner man" (Ephesians 3:16).

Remember, God's Revelation is Final. Those of you who read the first book called *Love & Respect* realize the same foundational verse exists: Ephesians 5:33. Why? This is God's last word to the church on marriage. There is no new word. If my dying dad called me to his deathbed saying, "Emerson, come close to me, I need to tell you something," you know these last words would linger in my heart and mind forever. The last words a person speaks hold the greatest significance. God's last word to the church on marriage—in terms of significance—is love and respect in Ephesians 5:33. Tomorrow, do not expect a new teaching to replace Ephesians 5:33. Thus, this workbook for *The Language of Love & Respect* moves you deeper into the application of love and respect to the mouth. No greater truth exists for couples! Please read Appendix II for an expanded explanation of this vital truth that God's revelation in the Bible about the mouth suffices. Sadly, too many forget, or never learn, the depth of His wisdom about communication in marriage.

If you wish to move through the study more quickly, e-mail me. Whether as a couple or facilitator of a small group, if you wish to move through this study at a quicker pace, please e-mail Emerson at CodeLight@loveandrespect.com and ask for the *Leader's Guide to a Quicker Study*.

If you are a Leader or Facilitator, refer to Appendix I. In the back of this workbook, you will find Suggestions for Group Leaders under Appendix I.

Are you ready? Then let's begin!

PART ONE: A BOOK WITHIN A BOOK

SESSION ONE

In preparation for this session, read the Introduction: "Is Communication Really the Key to Marriage?" and Part I, A Book Within a Book—Chapter One, "A Short Course on Love and Respect."

INTRODUCTION: IS COMMUNICATION REALLY THE KEY TO MARRIAGE?

The Biggest Problem: Communication

1. In a survey conducted by Focus on the Family for the Love and Respect Ministries, respondents were asked, "What was (and possibly still is) the biggest problem affecting your marriage?" For both men and women the biggest problem by far was lack of good communication.

   a. Why do you think communication problems in marriage surface as such a gigantic problem?

   _____

   _____

   _____

   _____

   b. In your opinion, what is the number one thing a couple should do to improve communication?

   _____

   _____

   _____

   _____

The Key: Mutual Understanding

2. Emerson writes, "It would be easy enough, then, to deduce that communication is the key to marriage, but I don't agree. To say that communication is the key to marriage is to assume that both spouses speak the same language. I have learned that, in fact, the wife speaks a 'love language' and the husband speaks a 'respect language.' They don't realize this, of course, but because he is speaking one kind of language (respect) and she is speaking another (love), there is little or no understanding and little or no communication" (p. 4).

   a. In Ephesians 5:33, God commands husbands to love and wives to respect. Do you agree with Emerson that this text suggests two languages, the language of love and the language of respect? Why do you agree or disagree?

   _____

   _____

   _____

   _____

   b. Reflect on your own marriage. As a wife, do unloving words leave you feeling misunderstood? As a husband, do disrespectful words leave you feeling misunderstood?

   _____

   _____

   _____

   _____

   c. When two people feel misunderstood, how does this hamper good communication?

   _____

   _____

   _____

   _____

Speaking with Love and Respect Works!

3. Emerson writes, "Husbands tell us they have learned what can happen when they use loving words to communicate with wives, and wives tell us they have been astounded

at the difference it makes when they use respectful words to communicate with their husbands."

a. As a wife, what do you feel when your husband speaks lovingly? As a husband, what do you feel when your wife speaks respectfully?

_____

_____

_____

_____

b. Why is the WAY we talk as important as WHAT we say?

_____

_____

_____

_____

Words Can Heal a Marriage

4. The Bible says, "The tongue of the wise brings healing" (Proverbs 12:18). Loving and respectful words have the power not only to create healthy communication but also to bring healing to the marriage.

a. On page 2, a wife says, "I start with an apology for my lack of respect." Men, share why this apology for being disrespectful can heal the heart of a husband.

_____

_____

_____

_____

b. On page 2, a husband says, "I am beginning to see how what I say and how I say it can feel hurtful to her." Women, share why this husband's willingness to speak loving words can bring healing to her heart.

_____

_____

_____

_____

Magic Formula?

5. The Bible says, "It's harder to make amends with an offended friend than to capture a fortified city. Arguments separate friends like a gate locked with iron bars" (Proverbs 18:19 NLT).

   a. According to this proverb, if you have offended each other, will healing come easily to your marriage if you express words of love or respect? Explain.

      _____

      _____

      _____

      _____

   b. On pages 2–3, read about some couples experiencing closed gates. Based on what these folks reported, why should you NOT declare the Love and Respect message a magic formula?

      _____

      _____

      _____

      _____

   c. Though a wife wounded her husband with disrespect (most often unintentionally) and though a husband wounded his wife with lack of love (most often unintentionally), why can a sincere apology speed up healing?

      _____

      _____

      _____

      _____

Clear Communication

In the best of marriages, healthy communication takes conscious effort. Each still needs to guard against sounding unloving and disrespectful.

6. The Clear Husband

A husband talks to his wife about her unbalanced checkbook. The husband, after studying the checkbook, CLEARLY COMMUNICATES with her where she mismanaged the money. She deposited $1,500 two times when she should have deposited $1,500 one time. Having spent the whole amount of $3,000, leaving them overdrawn by $1,500, they don't have the money to make this right.

Frustrated and angry with her, he points out where she made the mistake and what she needs to do to remedy the situation. He could not communicate more clearly! Tossing the checkbook on the desk, he exits in a huff and doesn't talk to her for the rest of the day.

a. Though this husband clearly communicates, rooted in his goodwill to help, why will he frustrate his wife? Will he end up frustrated by her reaction to him? What do you predict her reaction will look like?

_____

_____

_____

_____

b. A husband calls his wife childish when she shuts down in response to his anger and disgust. Why is judging a wife as childish ineffective?

_____

_____

_____

_____

c. Give some examples of how this husband could talk more lovingly in order to communicate effectively.

_____

_____

_____

_____

7. The Clear Wife

A husband takes care of the four children for the weekend while his wife participates in a women's retreat at a nearby Christian camp. When she returns, the husband gives a report about a fiasco that took place with Danny, the three-year-old. Danny, supposedly watched by the teen son, decides to hide downstairs behind the furnace. The teen chose to play a video game instead of closely watching Danny. When the husband gets off the phone, after talking to his ailing mother, he realizes Danny disappeared. Though he yells for Danny, the boy does not answer. The whole family searches the house and around the house and down the block, but still no Danny. Everyone panics. Eventually, Danny appears outside and tells them of his hiding place in the basement.

At the retreat several women talked about a toddler who wandered out of the house, went down the street, and was kidnapped by a sex offender recently released from prison. When this wife hears the report about Danny, fear comes over her. Her fear quickly turns to steaming anger. She yells at her husband, "You must pay attention! You cannot disengage. You must constantly check up on everyone." She tells him exactly what his parenting duties are. She CLEARLY COMMUNICATES how to manage these situations. Later this husband overhears his wife on the phone to her sister belittling him for his poor fathering.

a.   Though this wife clearly communicates, rooted in her goodwill to help, why will she frustrate her husband? Will she end up frustrated by his reaction to her? What do you predict his reaction to look like?

_____

_____

_____

_____

b.   A wife calls her husband childish when he shuts down in response to her belittling and disrespect. Why is judging a husband as childish ineffective?

_____

_____

_____

c.   Give some examples of how this wife could talk more respectfully in order to communicate effectively.

_____

_____

_____

_____

Who Moves First?

8. As you begin this study, an important question may arise—who moves first?

  a. Should the husband move first since Ephesians 5:33 begins with the husband loving his wife (5:33a) and the wife need only respect after her husband first loves her (5:33b)?

  _____

  _____

  _____

  b. Should the wife move first since the whole section on marriage begins with Ephesians 5:22 where the wife submits to her husband—submitting to his need to feel respected?

  _____

  _____

  _____

  c. Do you find yourself focusing more on your spouse's need to understand you, or your need to understand your spouse? If you see this more as your spouse's need, does that give your spouse all the power to change the relationship? Briefly write your thoughts about this.

  _____

  _____

  _____

  d. We live in a "victim" society. Is getting stuck in the victim mentality a temptation to you? Explain.

  _____

  _____

  _____

  e. If you see yourself as a victim of your spouse's bad behavior, does this allow you to justify disobedience to God's command in Ephesians 5:33? Do you think God sees you as a victim or someone who has the power to move first?

  _____

  _____

  _____

f. Are you willing to move first by learning your spouse's language, even if it appears your spouse is less willing to learn yours?

_____

_____

_____

If so, let's begin with a short course on how to communicate the love and respect way!

CHAPTER ONE: "A SHORT COURSE ON LOVE AND RESPECT"

In Chapter One, "A Short Course on Love and Respect," we receive a reminder that the Love and Respect approach to marriage consists of a person spinning on one of three cycles: the Crazy Cycle, the Energizing Cycle, or the Rewarded Cycle. As we work our way through this workbook, we address each of these cycles in depth. But first, let's take an honest assessment of our performance in each of these areas.

The Crazy Cycle

9. Many couples seem to spend most of their time on the Crazy Cycle, which is summed up like this:

WITHOUT LOVE, SHE REACTS WITHOUT RESPECT.
WITHOUT RESPECT, HE REACTS WITHOUT LOVE.

On page 5 Emerson writes: "As I pondered God's clear command (not suggestion) in Ephesians 5:33, I uncovered what I came to call the 'Love and Respect Connection.' I am commanded to love Sarah because she needs love; in fact, she 'speaks love.' Love is the language she understands. But when I speak to her in unloving ways, her tendency is to react with disrespectful words. Sarah is commanded to respect me because I need respect; in fact, I 'speak respect.' Respect is the language I understand. But when she speaks to me in disrespectful ways, my tendency is to react with unloving words. Round and round we would go in a Crazy Cycle, each saying things that were the exact opposite of what was needed!"

Can you identify with the Crazy Cycle? How?

_____

_____

_____

_____

A Bad Marriage?

10. All couples will experience the Crazy Cycle to some degree. This does not mean you have a bad marriage. Every marriage has some conflict and trouble. In fact, 1 Corinthians 7:28 states that when two people marry they "will face many troubles in this life" (NIV).

  a. How do you react to this statement by the apostle Paul in 1 Corinthians 7:28?

  _____

  _____

  _____

  _____

  b. Think of a time when you and your spouse got on the Crazy Cycle. What happened? Did you keep spinning? If necessary, review pages 11–19.

  _____

  _____

  _____

  _____

The Issue

11. Read the section "The 'Issue' Is Seldom the Real Issue" on page 14.

  a. What does Emerson mean by "the issue is seldom the real issue"? Have you experienced this?

  _____

  _____

  _____

  _____

b.   When the spirit of your spouse deflates and you ignore your wife's need to feel loved or your husband's need to feel respected, do you ignore the root issue and then spin on the Crazy Cycle? If this echoes your experience, explain why you are committed to find ways to stop this spinning.

_____

_____

_____

_____

The Unconditional

12. Read carefully the section entitled "Unconditional Really Means 'Unconditional' " on pages 16–19.

a.   In our love-saturated culture, everyone understands and expects unconditional love. On the other hand, what is your reaction to the phrase "unconditional respect"?

_____

_____

_____

b.   What does unconditional respect NOT mean? Do you agree or disagree with the following explanation by Emerson?

"Does unconditional respect mean a wife must respect evil behavior? Let me qualify what I mean by unconditional respect. Just as a husband is to come across lovingly even though his wife is not lovable, so a wife is to come across respectfully even though her husband is not respectable. This does not mean a wife must say, 'I respect the way you get angry and refuse to talk to me.' Such a statement is as silly as a husband saying, 'I love the way you nag and criticize me.' This is not about loving or respecting sinful behavior. This is about lovingly or respectfully confronting inappropriate behavior. Unconditional respect, like unconditional love, is all about how one sounds (tone of voice and word choice) and appears (facial expressions and physical actions). A husband may not deserve respect because he has not earned respect, but a wife's disrespect for him is ineffective long term—and not biblical. No husband responds to disrespectful attitudes any more than a wife responds to unloving attitudes" (p. 17).

_____

_____

_____

_____

c. Wives, even though 1 Peter 3:1–2 recommends unconditional respect as a way to win a disobedient husband, you may have fears giving your husband unconditional respect. If so, list some of your fears.

_____

_____

_____

_____

d. In Hosea 3:1, God calls Hosea the prophet to unconditionally love his adulterous wife. The Lord reveals that unconditional love qualifies as the best way to influence a wife to change her heart. If such love proved effective for Hosea, how much more will a goodwilled wife respond to the loving pursuits of a husband?

_____

_____

_____

_____

Husbands, do you have any concerns about giving your wife unconditional love? If so, list some of your concerns.

_____

_____

_____

_____

The Energizing Cycle

13. If you and your spouse can make a commitment to meet each other's deepest needs—unconditional love for her and unconditional respect for him—you can control the Crazy Cycle. However, even the happiest of couples can't stay off the

Crazy Cycle permanently. We're all human! To keep the Crazy Cycle in its cage, we need to get on the Energizing Cycle:

HIS LOVE MOTIVATES HER RESPECT.
HER RESPECT MOTIVATES HIS LOVE.

When applying this to communication we say: His loving words motivate her respectful words. Her respectful words motivate his loving words.

a. Wives, in light of the power of respectful words to influence the heart of a husband, why do you think some wives overlook God's method for motivating a husband?

_____

_____

_____

_____

b. Husbands, in light of the power of loving words to touch a wife's soul, why do you think some husbands overlook the power God has given them to motivate their wives?

_____

_____

_____

_____

LOVE = C-O-U-P-L-E

14. Husbands, read pages 21–23 on "C-O-U-P-L-E: A Checkup for Husbands." Review the acronym below.

C - Closeness: I am close—and not just when I want sex.

O - Openness: I open up to her, to talk and share, not acting angry or disinterested.

U - Understanding: I don't try to "fix" her but just listen—trying to be considerate when she's really upset.

P - Peacemaking: I practice and know the power in saying, "Honey, I'm really sorry."

L - Loyalty: I often assure her of my love and commitment.

E - Esteem: I honor and cherish her as first in importance.

a. Do an honest self-assessment on how you show love to your wife. What grade would you give yourself?

_____

_____

b. What grade do you think your wife would give you? Why? (Don't ask her at this point.)

_____

_____

RESPECT = C-H-A-I-R-S

15. Wives, carefully read the section on C-H-A-I-R-S: A Checkup for Wives (pp. 23–27). Review the acronym below.

C - Conquest: I recognize and thank him for his desire to work.
H - Hierarchy: I thank him for his motivation to protect and provide for me.
A - Authority: I acknowledge his desire to lead—and don't subvert his leadership.
I - Insight: I listen appreciatively to his ideas and the advice he wishes to offer.
R - Relationship: I value his desire for me to be his friend and stand shoulder to shoulder with him.
S - Sexuality: I respond to his need sexually; I don't deprive him.

a. Do an honest self-assessment on how well you show respect to your husband. What grade would you give yourself?

_____

_____

b. What grade do you think your husband would give you? Why? (Don't ask him at this time.)

_____

_____

Motivating Another

16. The key to motivating another person is meeting that person's deepest need.

    a. Do you agree with the above statement? Why or why not?

        _____

        _____

    b. Write down one of the principles from C-H-A-I-R-S or C-O-U-P-L-E that you believe most motivates your spouse. Think about something simple but specific you can do that will energize your mate. Make a mental note or put a reminder on your calendar to act on this.

        _____

        _____

The Rewarded Cycle

17. The final section of "A Short Course on Love and Respect" is the most important of all. In reality, there are times when understanding the Crazy Cycle and practicing the Energizing Cycle are not enough. Some wives will not show unconditional respect for their husbands no matter how well he unconditionally loves her. And some husbands will not show their wives unconditional love despite her best efforts at extending him unconditional respect. These couples live in some of the most difficult situations. The Rewarded Cycle gives us hope!

THE REWARDED CYCLE: REACHING YOUR ULTIMATE GOAL

HIS LOVE BLESSES REGARDLESS OF HER RESPECT. HER RESPECT BLESSES REGARDLESS OF HIS LOVE.

The Rewarded Cycle means that God blesses a husband who loves his wife regardless of her level of respect for him, and God blesses a wife who respects her husband regardless of his level of love for her. These blessings are the rewards God gives to those who love or respect a mate because of their own love and reverence for Christ. Christ Himself becomes the motivation for such action.

a. Write out your honest thoughts as you read this description of the Rewarded Cycle. Does it sound too lofty—or does it give you hope?

_____

_____

_____

_____

b. How fully do you believe that God will bless you if you love and respect in the midst of your difficulties?

_____

_____

_____

_____

God's Reward

18. Emerson writes, "When spouses come to me saying the Love and Respect Connection just isn't working, my advice is always the same: Don't give up.

"Keep doing your part because, in God's economy, no effort to obey Him is wasted. God intends to reward you even if your spouse is unresponsive. When you love or respect unconditionally regardless of the outcome, you are following God and His will for you. This is the Rewarded Cycle."

a. Have you thought much about God's intention to reward you for what you do? Read the following scriptures. Circle the words that reveal to whom these verses apply.

Revelation 22:12: "Behold, I am coming quickly, and My reward is with Me, to render to every man according to what he has done."

2 Job 1:8: "Watch yourselves, that you do not lose what we have accomplished, but that you may receive a full reward."

1 Corinthians 3:14: "If any man's work which he has built on it remains, he will receive a reward."

b. Do you believe the above verses apply to you personally? In other words, do you believe that God would actually reward you for showing love toward a disrespectful wife and respect toward an unloving husband? Or does God remain indifferent to the day-after-day existence in your marriage and only intend to reward great people like Billy Graham? Write out your thoughts.

_____

_____

_____

_____

_____

c. Jesus longs to say to every believer, "Well done, good and faithful servant. You have been faithful over a little; I will set you over much. Enter into the joy of your master" (Matthew 25:21 ESV). Because of your obedience to Ephesians 5:33, do you envision hearing Jesus say to you, "Well done, good and faithful servant"? Why or why not?

_____

_____

_____

_____

_____

The Prayer

19. To get the most from this study, open your heart to what the Lord wants to teach you. Pray the prayer of commitment below. In what part of this prayer do you most desire God's help? In what part of this prayer has God helped you the most?

A Prayer of Commitment

Dear Father,

I need You. I cannot love or respect perfectly, but I know You hear me when I ask You for help. First, please forgive me for the times I've been unloving or disrespectful. And help me to forgive my spouse for being unloving or disrespectful toward me. I open my heart to You, Father. I will not be fearful or angry at You or my spouse. I'm seeing myself and my spouse in a whole new light, and I will appreciate my spouse as being different, not wrong.

Lord, I also ask You to fill my heart with love and reverence for You. After all, this marriage is ultimately about You and me. It isn't about my spouse. Thank You for helping me both understand this truth and realize that my greatest reward will come from being a spouse as unto You.

Now prepare me this day for those inevitable moments of conflict. I especially ask You to put respect or love in my heart when I feel unloved or disrespected. I know there is no credit for loving or respecting when doing so is easy.

Finally, I believe that You hear my prayer, and I anticipate Your response. I thank You in advance for helping me take the next loving or respectful step in my marriage. I believe You will empower me, bless me, and even reward me for my effort as I approach marriage as unto You.

In the name of Jesus Christ,
Amen.

_____

_____

_____

_____

_____

_____

PART TWO: THREE VITAL TRUTHS FOR BETTER COMMUNICATION

SESSION TWO

—•◦•—

In this session, we begin Part II: Three Vital Truths for Better Communication. In preparation for this session, read the overview for Part II as well as Chapter Two, "In Marriage, the Mouth Matters" and Chapter Three, "Not Wrong, Just Different."

CHAPTER TWO: "IN MARRIAGE, THE MOUTH MATTERS"

The Mouth

1. What Jesus said becomes the basis of this chapter: The "mouth speaks from that which fills the heart" (Luke 6:45).

   a. In your opinion, what is Jesus saying?

   _____

   _____

   _____

   _____

   b. If you speak unloving or disrespectful words, what do these words tell about your heart?

   _____

   _____

   _____

   _____

c. If you speak loving or respectful words, what do these words evidence about your inner person?

_____

_____

_____

_____

The Swallowed Contact

2. Emerson tells the story of Sarah swallowing his contact lens when visiting his parents in Peoria (pp. 37–39). Both Emerson and Sarah ended up saying hurtful words to each other.

a. He comments, "Words have the power to hurt. Careless words, unloving words, disrespectful words, words spoken in anger or defensiveness" (p. 37). No doubt you have had similar episodes. At such moments, do you justify your hurtful words and blame your spouse for causing the unloving and disrespectful words?

_____

_____

_____

_____

b. Agree or disagree? If Sarah had not swallowed Emerson's contact, he would never have mouthed unloving words; therefore, Sarah caused Emerson's unkind remarks.

_____

_____

From the Heart

3. In marriage, most of us speak words that sound loving or respectful until under pressure!

   a. Do you recall the last time you felt under pressure and spoke unlovingly or disrespectfully to your spouse? Did you justify these unloving and disrespectful words by blaming your spouse?

   _____

   _____

   _____

   b. Does your spouse cause you to speak these unloving or disrespectful words? If so, does Jesus view you as an exception to Luke 6:45, when He says the "mouth speaks from that which fills the heart"?

   _____

   _____

   _____

   _____

Nobody Is Perfect

4. Someone objects: "Wait a minute, Emerson. Just because I slip up and use careless words doesn't necessarily mean that I don't have love or respect in my heart. Give me a break. I can't speak perfectly all the time. I can't always say just the right thing every moment of the day." That's a good point, and Sarah and I would agree that neither of us speaks perfectly all of the time. As James says, "If anyone does not stumble in what he says, he is a perfect man" (3:2).

   a. If you mess up with your words, does this mess-up automatically mean you have an unloving and disrespectful heart?

   _____

   _____

   _____

   _____

   _____

b. If you have blown it, how often do you apologize as evidence of your deepest heart, in that you did not intend to be unloving or disrespectful?

Very Often   Sometimes   Rarely

c. At this point, are you feeling overwhelmed by your personal inadequacies and feel like throwing in the towel on this workbook? If so, hang in there. Remember, James says none of us is perfect.

_____

_____

_____

_____

Your Success

5. Let's look at some of your successes.

a. Were you under pressure in your marriage over the last several weeks, yet you spoke lovingly or respectfully? Describe what you said.

_____

_____

_____

_____

b. What do these loving or respectful words say about your heart? Can you feel uplifted by the choices you are making? Why or why not?

_____

_____

_____

_____

The Tongue's Power

6. James also writes, "The tongue is a small thing, but what enormous damage it can do" (James 3:5 NLT).

a.   Can you expect your spouse to have confidence that you have love or respect in your heart if you speak words that damage the marriage?

_____

_____

_____

_____

b.   Where is God calling you to tone down some of your words that are unloving or disrespectful because of the damage such negative words are having?

_____

_____

_____

_____

c.   From the past, give an example of toning things down during "heated fellowship" to stop the damage to your marriage.

_____

_____

_____

_____

d.   In the group, have a moment of silence and each ask God for His help to stop the damaging talk.

The Pondering Heart

7. The Bible teaches that your heart can guide your mouth to speak appropriate words.

a.   What do these two verses say to you?

"The heart of the righteous ponders how to answer, but the mouth of the wicked pours out evil things" (Proverbs 15:28).

_____

_____

_____

_____

"The heart of the wise instructs his mouth and adds persuasiveness to his lips" (Proverbs 16:23).

_____

_____

_____

_____

b. Can you foresee a situation this week when you need to ponder how to answer and instruct your mouth so you can better persuade? How do you intend to talk?

_____

_____

_____

_____

Hot-Button Words

8. Emerson found that he and Sarah reacted to "hot-button" words (pp. 49–53).

Emerson comments, "After living and teaching Love and Respect for over eight years, Sarah and I are constantly amazed at the power of words and how they are spoken. And it's my educated guess that almost every couple has certain hot-button words or phrases that can cause trouble between them. For example, when Sarah is quite concerned (irritated) about something I have done or said (again), she uses the expression 'You *always* . . .' Whenever I hear 'You *always* . . . ,' I immediately lock up inside and think, 'That's not true. I don't *always* [do or say whatever Sarah is accusing me of].'

"On my side of the ledger, words I use that can set Sarah off are 'Honey, may I make a suggestion?' When I say these words, Sarah often hears a message of genuine disapproval. Why is this so? Because the thing about hot-button words is that, when they are spoken, the listener tends to expect the worst possible meaning."

a. Think about your marriage. What hot-button words exist? Write the hot-button words you hear from your spouse.

_____

_____

_____

b. Ponder for a moment, as Proverbs says, a better way to answer your spouse when hearing the hot-button words. Write down the better response. As you talk about the answers to these questions, do not blame and shame your spouse for his or her hot-button words. Focus on yourself, and share your new and wise responses to words that push your buttons.

_____

_____

_____

c. Do you know the hot-button words you use that set off your spouse? If not, choose a good moment to ask your spouse, but do not react defensively when he or she tells you! Write one or two sentences on how you plan to avoid using these words. If you are in a group and are willing to be accountable, share this commitment and ask a person in the group to ask you next time, privately, how you did.

_____

_____

_____

Wired Differently

9. A husband, in a study with many couples, writes, "Most of us have been married for a while, and it took a lot of hard experience before we came to realize the need to be aware of spousal differences and the need to be aware and sensitive to these differences. I think that we all realize how much easier things would have been if we had the tools that you talk about when we began our marriages, or better yet when we were dating."

a. Husband, how do you rate your awareness of speaking in sensitive ways (with words of love) to your feminine wife? Wife, how do you rate your awareness of speaking in sensitive ways (with words of respect) to your masculine husband?

Very Aware   Somewhat Aware   Clueless

b. The Crazy Cycle can happen anywhere and anytime because of our wiring as men and women. When those different wires get crossed, the communication sparks can fly! Have you been on the Crazy Cycle too often because you are not discerning these honest differences? If yes, explain a possible remedy to reduce the spinning.

_____

_____

_____

_____

c. Why do you believe God created husband and wife to be so different in the way they talk? What are you learning about not letting these differences result in communication problems?

_____

_____

_____

_____

CHAPTER THREE: "NOT WRONG, JUST DIFFERENT"

A popular analogy that we use at our Love and Respect conferences describes the differences between men and women as pink and blue. Women look at the world through pink sunglasses, while men look at the same world through blue sunglasses—and, believe me, they do not always see the same thing! The sexes must discern that neither is wrong, but simply different—in body function, outlook, and perspective.

Pink and blue perceptions affect not only seeing but also hearing. Using the same pink and blue analogy, women hear with pink hearing aids, and men hear with blue hearing aids. When it comes to communication between the sexes, each can hear the same words but different messages.

Who's Right?

10. Read the story in the section "Next Time Ask about the Really Important Stuff!" on pages 56–58.

a. Can you identify with the challenges that Emerson and Sarah face?

_____

_____

_____

_____

b. How does this story illustrate that husbands and wives are not wrong, just different?

_____

_____

_____

_____

c. How might you apply Romans 15:7 to prevent disagreements from escalating into feuds between pink and blue? "Accept one another, just as Christ also accepted us."

_____

_____

_____

_____

Male and Female

11. It is no coincidence that the first chapter of the Bible quickly establishes that God created male and female (Genesis 1:27: "God created man in His own image . . . male and female He created them") or that the second chapter of Genesis elaborates on His creation as He places Adam in the garden, with orders to "cultivate and keep it." Then, noting it is not good for Adam to be alone, God creates a woman to join him and be his helper. All goes well in paradise until sin enters, and then everything changes.

a. Read the following scriptures and record what the Word says about the differences between men and women. (Read the section "In the Beginning, God Created Them Pink and Blue" on pages 60–62 for helpful insights.)

Genesis 3:16–19: "To the woman He said, 'I will greatly multiply your pain in childbirth, in pain you will bring forth children; yet your desire will be for your husband, and he will rule over you.'

"Then to Adam He said, 'Because you have listened to the voice of your wife, and have eaten from the tree about which I commanded you, saying, 'You shall not eat from it'; cursed is the ground because of you; in toil you will eat of it all the days of your life. Both thorns and thistles it shall grow for you, and you will eat the plants of the field; by the sweat of your face you will eat bread, till you return to the ground, because from it you were taken; for you are dust, and to dust you shall return.' "

1 Peter 3:7: "You husbands in the same way, live with your wives in an understanding way, as with someone weaker, since she is a woman."

Jeremiah 30:6: "Ask now, and see if a male can give birth."

1 Thessalonians 2:7: "We proved to be gentle among you, as a nursing mother tenderly cares for her own children."

1 Corinthians 16:13: "Stand firm in the faith, act like men, be strong."

Nehemiah 4:14: "Fight for your brothers, your sons, your daughters, your wives and your houses."

b. Summarize what you learned about males and females from these verses.

_____

_____

_____

_____

Equally Valued

12. While it is clear from Scripture that God has created us with distinct male and female differences, it is also important to note that God views us as equal in value. Paul pens, "There is neither male nor female; for you are all one in Christ Jesus" (Galatians 3:28). In other words, God does not make us unisex or androgynous after we come to Christ. But God does make us one in the sense that we are equal in the eyes of the Father.

a. What does it mean to be equally valued in God's eyes?

_____

_____

_____

_____

b.   Some have difficulty grasping that men and women differ. After all, if in the eyes of God equality exists, then a man and woman must be identical. The feminist movement often taught that except for a little biology, men and women equal one another in identical ways. However, the biological differences go deeper into the psyche than some acknowledge. Emerson writes, "Have you ever thought about how basic biology and anatomy affect the mind, will, and emotions? These three components combine to become what is called a person's 'soul.' We can quibble over what exactly is the soul, but in my opinion, mind, will, and emotions certainly have plenty to do with it. The question before us, then, is 'Because of different biology and anatomy, do men and women think differently, prefer differently, and feel differently in their very souls?' " (See the section entitled "Vive La Différence!" on page 63 for added insight.) Have you thought much about these things? Jot down some of your thoughts.

_____

_____

_____

_____

Extending Empathy

13. Read the sections entitled "Pornography Is Basically a Male Problem" and "How the Pain of PMS Affects Her Soul" on pages 64–67.

a.   What are your thoughts and feelings as you read the sections on pornography and PMS?

_____

_____

_____

_____

b.   Is it difficult for you to allow your spouse to be different when it comes, for example, to the temptations men experience related to pornography and the trials women experience related to PMS?

_____

_____

_____

_____

c. No one should justify the sexual sin of a husband or the sinful outbursts of anger by a wife. But can you extend empathy to the struggles males and females have in overcoming these weaknesses? Can you, wife, recognize God has not made you as visually oriented as your husband, so pornography does not tempt you as it does him? Can you, husband, recognize God has not made you with a menstrual cycle as a man, therefore PMS does not overwhelm you as a monthly test?

_____

_____

_____

_____

d. If you have unmarried children, consider the future when they are married. Would you want your daughter-in-law to harshly judge your son because she does not struggle with the same things with which he struggles? Would you want your son-in-law to harshly judge your daughter because he does not struggle with the same things with which she struggles?

_____

_____

_____

_____

Not Wrong, Just . . .

14. Except for the clear immoral challenges like lust leading to adultery and rage leading to violence, there are daily personal preferences (i.e., her preference to talk and his preference to be shoulder to shoulder without talking) that differ between husband and wife.

a. Emerson encourages us to use the phrase "NOT WRONG, JUST DIFFERENT" to look at our mates with new eyes. Jot down an area in your marriage where you and your spouse have struggled over a difference between personal preferences based on your maleness or femaleness (i.e., watching a chick flick versus a guy movie). Think back to a heartbreaking conflict that was rooted in an honest male and female difference about a gender preference. On reflection about this disagreement, would you concur with the slogan "Not wrong, just different"? How will this phrase help you during future conflicts?

_____

_____

_____

_____

b.   Research has confirmed that women speak 20,000 words a day and men speak 7,000 words a day. Can you give grace to your spouse in this area, respecting him for his preference to not talk at times and loving her for her preference to talk at times?

_____

_____

_____

_____

c.   Take time right now to ask God to give you new eyes with which to accept your spouse's male or female differences.

SESSION THREE

———

CHAPTER FOUR: "CAN YOU TRUST YOUR SPOUSE'S GOODWILL? (CAN YOUR SPOUSE TRUST YOURS?)"

In preparation for this session, read Chapter Four: "Can You Trust Your Spouse's Goodwill? (Can Your Spouse Trust Yours?)"

So far we have covered two vital truths that can help the Love and Respect couples develop mutual understanding and good communication: the mouth matters, and husbands and wives are not wrong, just different. The third and vital truth focuses on another simple but crucial concept: both of you must see each other as goodwilled persons. When one or both of you see the other as goodwilled, good things happen in your marriage!

Two Scenarios

1. When marital conflicts arise, they leave each person asking this question: "Does my spouse have goodwill toward me right now?" Read the following two scenarios and give your opinion on them.

Scenario 1:

> You have to leave early in the morning, and you haven't had time to fill the car with gas. Your spouse promises to go out and take care of it while you do some last-minute packing and reports. The next day, as you are rushing to leave, you find the gauge on "Empty," and you feel a surge of anger. In the next few moments, you can choose to believe your spouse "just doesn't care" and has ill will toward you (or lacks goodwill), or you can choose to believe your spouse made an honest mistake because you know she (or he) does not normally neglect a known need.

a. Can you identify with this scenario? How would you respond?

_____

_____

_____

_____

Scenario 2:

Or what about those times when your spouse does something that is consciously nasty or maybe even a little hateful (perhaps to "teach you a lesson")? To stay with the didn't-fill-the-tank example, suppose you had come home late for dinner, hadn't called, and then forgot to pick up what he or she wanted at the store. Perhaps your spouse is so angry he or she decides to let your gas tank go unfilled as payback for your careless behavior. I have heard of all kinds of payback couples pull on each other, particularly if they entered the Crazy Cycle to any degree. One couple had a spat, and both were so angry they hadn't spoken to each other all day or evening. Before going to bed he wrote her a note and left it on her pillow: "If I don't hear the alarm, please wake me up at 5:30 a.m. since you get up at 5:00. I have an important breakfast meeting." At 7:00 the next morning, he finally woke up and was in disbelief. His wife had not awakened him! As he angrily rolled out of bed, he noticed her note on the nightstand: "Wake up! It's 5:30 a.m."

Almost all married couples have encounters that lead to reactions designed to send the message: "You hurt me, so I am going to hurt you so you will stop hurting me!" Does this sort of encounter mean that one or both of you lack basic goodwill toward the other? Of course not. Your angry spouse might temporarily not wish you well, but these exceptions don't do away with the rule, and the rule says, "I will choose to believe in my spouse's goodwill when he or she does me wrong, whether unintentional or intentional."

b. What are your thoughts on this scenario?

_____

_____

_____

c. These situations leave you with a choice to decide if your spouse has goodwill. When the Crazy Cycle happens, what would it take for you to make a choice to trust your spouse's goodwill?

_____

_____

_____

d. What results when labeling your spouse ill-willed when s/he has goodwill?

_____

_____

_____

Emerson's Discovery

2. When counseling Christian couples, Emerson often wondered if couples did, indeed, have goodwill toward one another. As he turned to the Scriptures for help, he discovered 1 Corinthians 7:32–34.

a. Read the section entitled "Can Goodwill Be Overlooked?" on pages 74–75. Imagine Emerson counseling you. Would you answer his questions the same as those he counseled in the story?

_____

_____

_____

_____

b. Give your opinion on the following: In the normal flow of marriage, neither spouse gets up in the morning thinking, *How can I displease my mate or show I don't care about my spouse's needs?* Nonetheless, as the day goes by, things happen. Without realizing it, he may sound harsh and unloving, and she reacts with disrespect. Or she may treat him with disrespect in one of a dozen different little ways, and he reacts in an unloving manner. Conflict occurs, during which spouses get nasty with each other. Both have goodwill, but it doesn't seem that way!

_____

_____

_____

_____

Goodwill Defined

3. Emerson uses the term *goodwill* when talking about husbands and wives. But what is goodwill? A simple definition of goodwill is "the intention to do good toward the other person."

   a. Do you agree with this definition?

   _____

   _____

   b. Does goodwill always include good follow-through?

   Read Matthew 26:36–41 and consider the disciples in the Garden of Gethsemane. As you recall, instead of praying and supporting Jesus throughout the night during His time of need in the Garden of Gethsemane, Peter, James, and John fell asleep. Even so, Jesus said to them, "The spirit is willing, but the flesh is weak" (v. 41). Jesus looked past their weakness, into their willing spirit. How does this serve to remind you that your spouse can have goodwill but not good follow-through?

   _____

   _____

   _____

   c. When your spouse fails to follow through on good intentions, your definition of goodwill must include the idea that goodwilled people do not mean harm; they do not intend real evil toward one another. Does your definition of goodwill include this idea? Why or why not?

   _____

   _____

   _____

   _____

Poor Follow-Through

4. The apostle Paul captured the reality of good intentions but poor follow-through when he wrote about his own struggles with the flesh in Romans 7:19: "I don't do the good things I want to do. I keep on doing the evil things I don't want to do" (NIrV).

   a. Can you identify with Paul? If so, can you give your spouse the same benefit you hope your spouse gives to you?

   _____

   _____

   _____

   b. During conflict, what would happen in your marriage if you said to yourself, "Though my spouse has goodwill about loving/respecting me, I know that at times my spouse struggles to follow through on his/her good intentions, and that's okay"?

   _____

   _____

   _____

   _____

   c. Share a time when your spouse failed to meet your expectation for love/respect and you overlooked the failure. You knew other factors existed that made it tough for your spouse to meet your expectations.

   _____

   _____

   _____

   _____

   d. Wife, your husband unintentionally speaks in a way that feels unloving to you. Will you give him grace knowing that you unintentionally speak in ways that feel disrespectful to him?

   _____

   Husband, your wife unintentionally speaks in a way that feels disrespectful to you. Will you give her grace knowing that you unintentionally speak in ways that feel unloving to her?

   _____

The Wicked Heart

5. Sinful people can have goodwill.

   Emerson writes: "Wherever I teach about goodwill, I am asked, 'How do you reconcile the concept of goodwill with the total depravity of the human heart?' Some people go so far as to say, 'We can't have goodwill because of our sinful heart,' and they quote Jeremiah 17:9 to prove their point: 'The heart is deceitful and desperately wicked. Who can know it?' (KJV). I believe what Jeremiah teaches, but I also believe what Jesus teaches: 'The seed in the good soil, these are the ones who have heard the word in an honest and *good heart*, and hold it fast, and bear fruit with perseverance' (Luke 8:15, italics mine). The obvious question becomes, 'If the heart is "deceitful and desperately wicked," how can a person have an "honest and good heart"?' The answer has two sides: the side created in the image of God and the fallen side corrupted by sin. As I just mentioned, when Jesus said, 'The spirit is willing but the flesh is weak,' I understand this to mean we have a spiritual side that longs to do what is good, based on the moral law implanted in us by God, but we have a carnal side that pulls us into sin."

   a. Based on what Emerson wrote, how does goodwill square with a deceitful and wicked heart?

   _____

   _____

   _____

   _____

   b. Is Emerson justifying your spouse's sinful words by claiming s/he is goodwilled? Why or why not?

   _____

   _____

   _____

   _____

   c. When your spouse confesses sinful speech, how is your forgiveness made easier when looking into his or her deeper spirit where s/he longs to do what is right?

   _____

   _____

   _____

   _____

Biblical Goodwill

6. The Bible teaches the reality of goodwill and expects goodwill. Paul writes, "With good will render service, as to the Lord, and not to men" (Ephesians 6:7).

   a. In Ephesians 6:5–9 Paul addresses slaves and masters. On the one hand, he instructs slaves to render service with goodwill (v. 7), and on the other hand he commands masters to "do the same things to them" (v. 9). Since suffering slaves served with goodwill, can you serve with goodwill? Why?

   _____

   _____

   _____

   _____

   b. Explain what you think would happen if you told your spouse you have goodwill.

   _____

   _____

   _____

   _____

Pink and Blue

7. Emerson writes, "I often hear from a wife who feels her marriage is utterly hopeless and that her husband lacks goodwill. She draws this conclusion because he reacts in ways that she would not—and if she reacted in such a fashion, it would mean that she lacks goodwill and is cruel." The same idea applies to a husband. "I would never talk to anyone the way my wife talks to me, especially when she sighs, rolls her eyes, sours her face, points her finger and tells me I am not the man she thought I was" (p. 85).

   a. Though your spouse reacts to you in ways you would not react, can you assume such a reaction exhibits more of a pink and blue difference than ill-will? What happens when you do not assume this difference is showing a male and female bent, and you refuse to extend grace?

   _____

   _____

   _____

   _____

b. If you made this positive assumption and gave grace on a regular basis, how might this change your marriage for the better?

_____

_____

_____

_____

The Choice

8. Emerson makes this comment: "I will choose to believe in my spouse's goodwill." Along with Emerson, you, too, have opportunities to make this choice. Read the following statements and decide how you would respond if you chose to believe your spouse has goodwill:

a. Husbands: Your wife says something like, "Sex and food—that is all you want from me!" Though you feel disrespected by your wife's words, do you recognize she intends for you to reassure her that you love her, for her? Why or why not?

_____

_____

_____

_____

b. Wives: Your husband says something like, "I can never be good enough! You are never satisfied!" Though you feel unloved by your husband's words, do you recognize he intends for you to reassure him that you respect him, for him? Why or why not?

_____

_____

_____

_____

c. This week will you choose to trust your mate's goodwill when you find yourself spinning on the Crazy Cycle? If not, what holds you back?

_____

_____

_____

Evil Will

9. Scripture attests that we live in a fallen world in which some people intend to do wrong.

   a. What do these two Scripture passages mean to you? In Proverbs 2:16–17 we learn that a wife can become a wayward woman "who has left the partner of her youth and ignored the covenant she made before God" (NIV). And in Malachi 2:13–14, the prophet tells wayward men that God no longer honors their offerings and instead is "acting as the witness between you and the wife of your youth, because you have broken faith with her, though she is your partner, the wife of your marriage covenant" (NIV).

   _____

   _____

   _____

   _____

   b. Emerson knows firsthand that spouses do evil things to their mates. Read his personal story about his mom and dad on page 78 and record your thoughts and feelings.

   _____

   _____

   _____

   _____

   c. In his concluding statement on pages 78–79, Emerson says: "My mother never minimized his actions. She never went into denial, saying he didn't know what he was doing. At the same time—despite the painful, unnerving episodes that stick in my mind—neither my mother nor I, young as I was, ever concluded that Dad was evil willed. We chose to believe that, while Dad had committed evil acts, he was not evil willed." What is your opinion on what Emerson shared about his parents?

   _____

   _____

   _____

   _____

Taking Snapshots

10. If you have doubts about your mate's deepest heart, ask yourself, "How does the Lord view my mate?"

    a. As you recall, Judas betrayed Jesus and Peter denied Him (see Matthew 26; Matthew 25:1–5; and John 21). However, the spirit of Judas differs from the spirit of Peter. Judas did what he did from a deceptive spirit whereas Peter did what he did because of momentary fear and doubt.

        What harm comes to a marriage when one judges a spouse as a Judas when the Lord sees this person as a Peter?

        _____

        _____

        _____

        _____

    b. In the section entitled "Look at Your Spouse as Jesus Would" you read of the importance of distinguishing between a snapshot of your spouse (at a weak, sinful moment) and the movie of your spouse's life. If you misrepresent your spouse by holding up a snapshot and playing a sound bite, why does this damage your marriage? Why must you choose to refuse to misrepresent your spouse?

        _____

        _____

        _____

        _____

    c. Have you ever had someone take a snapshot of your behavior and draw broad condemning conclusions about your whole character? If so, how did this feel?

        _____

        _____

        _____

        _____

Note Writing

11. When it comes to acknowledging a spouse's goodwill, it can feel awkward. Consider writing your spouse a note to express thoughts that seem too difficult to say. You may want to use the following verbatim or adapt it to your own way of saying things.

    Both of us have goodwill. I am sure God wants us to stop this petty craziness caused by our snapshot judgments. We have both acted defensively but ended up offending each other. It's time to try to understand each other and forgive each other. Will you forgive me for my actions that have triggered the Crazy Cycle?

    a. How might your spouse respond to this note? How would you respond if your spouse wrote this to you?

    _____

    _____

    _____

    _____

    b. If you choose to believe your spouse has goodwill, you can see him or her as a friend or an ally, even if you become irritated or angry with one another. What can you do, specifically, this week to build on your friendship with your spouse?

    _____

    _____

    _____

    _____

12. As we close this section on vital truths for better communication, let's review the three truths that work together to help you and your spouse build mutual understanding:

    First, your mouth matters, and what comes out of your mouth depends on a heart committed to living out Love and Respect in your marriage.

    Second, neither of you is wrong. You are just different from each other. Your pink and blue perspectives shade and influence every communication that passes between you.

    And third, each of you must see the other as a goodwilled person even when— especially when—the Crazy Cycle starts to spin.

Which of these three has impacted you the most and why?

_____

_____

_____

_____

PART THREE: THE CRAZY CYCLE: A RELENTLESS ENEMY OF MARITAL COMMUNICATION

SESSION FOUR

———⟨⟩———

In this session, we start Part III, The Crazy Cycle: A Relentless Enemy of Marital Communication. In preparation for this session, read the overview for Part III and Chapter Five, "Decode—and Stop the Crazy Cycle" and Chapter Six, "Ouch! You're Stepping on My Air Hose!"

The Crazy Cycle is a clever, relentless enemy. No married couple gets off the Crazy Cycle for good, but you can avoid it or jump off by using the basic skills and techniques described in the following chapters.

CHAPTER FIVE: "DECODE—AND STOP THE CRAZY CYCLE"

Remember, the Crazy Cycle says: without love a wife reacts in ways that feel disrespectful to her husband (which she is not intending), and without respect a husband reacts in ways that feel unloving (which he is not intending).

The Airport Story

1. Even "experts" like Emerson and Sarah must stay alert lest they fall victims to the Crazy Cycle. Read the airport story at the beginning of Chapter Five (p. 89).

   a. Write a statement about what "caused" them to spin on the Crazy Cycle.

   _____

   _____

   _____

b. What did they do to stop it from spinning out of control?

_____

_____

_____

_____

c. In what ways can you identify with this story?

_____

_____

_____

_____

Calling a Truce

2. Emerson writes that they have called a truce in the battle of the sexes.

   a. Though tension still arises between them, what do they do to stop the Crazy Cycle? Choose the right answer below:

   1. Emerson and Sarah avoid talking about the conflicts. By steering clear of an open discussion about the deeper issues of love and respect, they form a truce. Nevertheless, during the truce they both sulk as a way of punishing each other. They dwell together as unhappy, decent people.

   2. Emerson and Sarah reach truces by exhausting one another in arguments. After locking horns for a period, with the ultimate goal of pointing out the other's lack of love or respect, they grow weary bumping heads. Too tired to fight, they call a cease-fire. They either apologize or emotionally shut down until recovering to hurl the next verbal hand grenade.

   3. Sarah no longer labels Emerson an unloving blue dummy and Emerson does not profile Sarah a disrespectful pink basket case. Both recognize that in most conflicts neither is wrong, just different. Further, neither castigates the other as ill-willed. These new views allow them to tackle issues and slow down the Crazy Cycle. They see the other as an ally, not an enemy.

   b. Which of these three methods do you primarily use to call a "truce"?

   _____

Not Wrong, Just Different.

3. Please read Romans 14.

In this passage, God reveals a major truth to His people. When conflicts arise, gray areas exist in which neither side is morally wrong. For example, we see that worshiping God on the Jewish Sabbath (Friday night) continued as the preferred holy day of some. But worshiping on the Lord's Resurrection Day (Sunday morning) became the chosen holy day of others. Paul is clear: neither is wrong, just different. Or, a believer converted from kosher Judaism could eat pork. Still, because of upbringing many Jews did not feel free to eat bacon, lettuce, and tomato sandwiches. But a Gentile converted to Christianity could eat pork chops. Paul teaches neither is wrong, just different.

God's call to the early church, as today, demanded that believers stop their damning judgments of those with differing convictions in the gray areas. This applies to marriage too! God expects a married couple to accept their different convictions in the gray areas without judging or attacking one another. Preferences, opinions, and convictions can hold great importance to you but carry little value to your mate. For example, a husband wants to save extra money for retirement but the wife believes their retirement plan is already sufficient. Instead, she wants to use the money to improve the value of their home. This spawns a conflict. Yet, neither is wrong, just different.

When a tug-of-war starts, ask yourself: "Is this a 'Thus saith the Lord' issue resulting in my spouse committing sin? For example, is my spouse clearly transgressing one of the Ten Commandments (Exodus 20)? Or, is this a gray area about which we have an honest difference of opinion?"

When gray-area conflicts arise between Emerson and Sarah, they seek to refrain from judging the other as wrong. This doesn't mean one gives in without a debate! Strong disagreements arise. But here's the deal. Neither condemns the other because of differing convictions.

a. In your marriage, where have you accepted honest differences as a way of stopping the Crazy Cycle?

_____

_____

_____

_____

b.   Right now, are you banging heads on a gray-area issue and judging your spouse as wrong? Is the Lord judging your spouse in the same way?

_____

_____

_____

_____

Back to the Airport

4. The airport story illustrates that strong preferences arise. Sarah has strong sentiments about matters of love, which Emerson by nature doesn't feel as she feels. And Emerson has strong views about respectful treatment during conflict, which Sarah by nature doesn't see as Emerson sees. So, to communicate, Sarah and Emerson (and you too!) must learn to decode these outlooks, and accept and appreciate them.

a.   Sarah wants to eat together as a means for talking, connecting, and igniting the feelings of love between them. She cannot believe Emerson fails to see this. Hurt, Sarah negatively reacts to Emerson for not picking up on her invitation to connect. To Emerson her indirect and unclear expectation strikes him as unfair. Making him guess registers in his mind as a little disrespectful. Of course, when he pulls back, she feels more unloved! Round and round it goes!

Husbands, do you decode your wife's desire to connect with you and to feel your love? Or, do you judge her as disrespectful and wrong for her unclear expectations? Why?

_____

_____

_____

_____

b.   Emerson did not pick up on Sarah's indirectness about getting something to eat as her request to "connect." So, he cannot believe she would get upset with him over an honest misunderstanding when her expectations were unclear. But Sarah is in disbelief that Emerson fails to recognize her desire. Further, her indirect approach was rooted in her desire to not be "bossy"—can't he see she was just trying to be respectful? Of course, when she stomps off in a huff, he feels more disrespect from her. Round and round it goes!

Wives, do you decode your husband's desire to feel respected during times of misunderstanding in the same way that you desire to feel loved and respected? Or, do you judge him as arrogant for his desire to feel respected, and as unloving for not "getting it"? Explain.

_____

_____

_____

_____

Presumption

5. Proverbs 13:10 says, "Through presumption comes nothing but strife."

   a. What comes to pass when you wrongly presume? For example, what results when you wrongly think your spouse is aggravating you intentionally? Give a specific example.

   (For additional commentary about presumption, read the sections "Where Did You Get These Hamburgers?" and " 'Can We Talk?' Would Put Me on Red Alert.")

   _____

   _____

   _____

   _____

   b. In the airport, when Sarah felt unloved and Emerson felt disrespected, which of the following statements should they live by?

   1. "Though I feel unloved/disrespected, my spouse does not intend to treat me this way."

   2. "Because I feel unloved/disrespected, my spouse intends to mistreat me."

"You Are So Critical!"

6. In the final section of Chapter Five, entitled "Listening and Decoding: Twin Tools for Better Communication" (p. 100), read the email story.

a. How do the twin tools of listening and decoding save the day for the "critical" wife?

_____

_____

_____

_____

b. Why is "listening" not enough? Why is "decoding" her husband's meaning and intent—without exploding in anger—crucial?

_____

_____

_____

_____

c. What would have happened if she had verbally assaulted him with words of disdain?

_____

_____

_____

d. Explain what would change in your marriage if you assumed that your spouse was not reacting in unloving or disrespectful ways on purpose.

_____

_____

_____

_____

e. How does James 1:19 help prevent the Crazy Cycle? "Be quick to listen, but slow to speak and slow to become angry" (TEV).

_____

_____

_____

_____

CHAPTER SIX: "OUCH! YOU'RE STEPPING ON MY AIR HOSE!"

The Deflating Spirit

7. Emerson uses the analogy of an air hose leading to a big tank labeled "Love" for women and "Respect" for men to illustrate how we need love or respect like we need air to breathe. Unfortunately, in marriage we step on the other's air hose!

   a. Think of a time when you said something that stepped on your spouse's air hose. When their spirit deflated, did you notice or did you get distracted by the negative reaction toward you?

   _____

   _____

   _____

   _____

   b. Husband, why do your unloving ways cause the spirit of your wife to deflate?

   _____

   _____

   _____

   _____

   Wife, why do your disrespectful ways cause the spirit of your husband to deflate?

   _____

   _____

   _____

   _____

   c. When your spouse steps on your air hose, describe what you feel. Does your spouse feel the same way? Do you empathize with one another?

   _____

   _____

   _____

   _____

Asking Your Spouse to Help

8. When your spirit deflates, courageously and honestly communicate (with love and respect) the feelings of your heart.

    a. Wife, what would happen if you said the following? "I know you have goodwill and did not intend to step on my air hose. But will you help me? What just happened felt unloving to me."

_____

_____

_____

        Husband, what would happen if you said the following? "I know you have goodwill and did not intend to step on my air hose. But will you help me? What just happened felt disrespectful to me."

_____

_____

_____

    b. If your spouse said this to you, what would be your reaction?

_____

_____

_____

The Real Root Issue

9. Remember, when you speak stinging words that cause an issue, that issue usually gives way to a deeper issue of love or respect. The cutting words feel disrespectful to a husband and he deflates, and hurtful words feel unloving to a wife and she deflates.

    a. Do you remember a conflict over some topic when that issue turned into a love or respect issue? Explain.

_____

_____

_____

b. Did the spirit of your spouse deflate? If so, describe how you responded, and why.

_____

_____

_____

Strength Versus Vulnerability

10. Judgment happens when the stronger judges the more vulnerable. The stronger feels smarter or better. The stronger looks down on the other, feeling superior.

    a. Agree or Disagree?

    1. A husband judges his wife based on his strengths and her vulnerabilities.

       For example, a wife feels vulnerable when getting a diet book. "Body image" issues are more "touchy" to her than they are to her husband. In the diet book, a wife hears the message: "I do not accept you, approve of you, or love you unless you look like a Dallas Cowboy cheerleader." If she gave her husband a diet book, he would not hear this message! Instead he'd reply, "Thanks. What's for dinner?"

       Because God gave a husband natural strengths in areas where his wife has vulnerabilities, it is easy for a husband to judge his wife as childish when she deflates over things that don't deflate him.

    2. A wife judges her husband based on her strengths and his vulnerabilities.

       For example, a husband feels vulnerable when getting a third marriage book to read. In the third marriage book, a husband hears the message: "I do not accept you, approve of you, or respect you unless you change right now!" If he gave her a third marriage book she would not hear this message! She'd reply, "Wow, would you like to read it together? Can we start tonight?"

       Because God gave a wife natural strengths in areas where her husband has vulnerabilities, it is easy for a wife to judge her husband as childish when he deflates over things that don't deflate her.

b. When the spirit of your spouse deflates, how effective is saying, "Oh, grow up. You are being childish"? Do you pass judgment based on your strengths? If so, what will you do to stop such arrogant judging?

_____

_____

_____

_____

Flight, Fight, or God's Way?

11. Emerson writes: "About now it's possible that some spouses may be thinking, *This decoding and avoiding air hoses is an awful lot of work.* You're right. There is work involved. . . . But it is actually less work than you might think. You can decide not to bother decoding your spouse's words, and you can forget to worry about your spouse's air hose. But realize you are *already* in a pattern of some kind, responding to your spouse in some fashion, quite possibly jumping to conclusions and sidestepping deeper issues. Guess what? You end up spending just as much—if not more!—time and energy getting angry, withdrawing, pouting, accusing, defending, worrying—and losing sleep" (p. 115).

a. Do you think communicating in the ways this book recommends requires too much work? If so, what are the alternatives?

_____

_____

_____

_____

b. If you avoid the real issue of love or respect (flight) or become volatile when feeling unloved or disrespected (fight), what result does this have on communication?

_____

_____

_____

_____

c. Compared to ignoring your spouse or yelling at your spouse, how much tougher is it to ask, "Did I come across unloving/disrespectful?" or saying, "I know you are goodwilled but that felt unloving/disrespectful"? If you are in a group, share how you are tackling the real issue of love or respect.

_____

_____

_____

_____

Prevent Marital Forest Fires

12. You can apply a technique that prevents spinning on the Crazy Cycle by staying off your spouse's air hose.

a. Ask yourself this question:

Husbands: "Is what I am about to do or say going to feel unloving to her?"
Wives: "Is what I am about to do or say going to feel disrespectful to him?"

b. In the space below, note what changes occurred when you tried this technique. Did your speech or actions change? Did your spouse's behavior toward you change?

_____

_____

_____

_____

Lighten Up!

13. To keep the Crazy Cycle in its cage, remember that there is "a right time to . . . laugh" (Ecclesiastes 3:4 MSG).

a. One couple says, "We have agreed to give each other the freedom to say, in effect: 'You're crossing the line and squashing my spirit with how you're saying what you're saying.' Neither of us actually uses that line as a quote. Instead, I grab my throat and act like I'm choking, and my wife tells me I'm stomping on her air hose" (p. 111).

Can you do this in your marriage? Why or why not?

_____

_____

_____

_____

b.   How do you keep things light when conflicts arise?

_____

_____

_____

_____

SESSION FIVE

―――※☼※―――

CHAPTER SEVEN: "FORGIVENESS: THE ULTIMATE STRATEGY FOR HALTING THE CRAZY CYCLE"

In preparation for this session, read Chapter Seven, "Forgiveness: The Ultimate Strategy for Halting the Crazy Cycle."

In Session Four, we looked at two important communication strategies for stopping the Crazy Cycle: learn to decode each other's messages; and don't step on each other's air hose. In this session, we will consider the third and most important strategy for stopping the Crazy Cycle: forgive each other as Christ forgave you.

Mistreatment

1. When your spouse responds in unloving or disrespectful ways (the Crazy Cycle!), you will probably feel mistreated.

   a. Husband, when your wife yells at you for something upsetting her, why do you feel mistreated, disrespected, and resentful?

   _____

   _____

   _____

   _____

   b. Wife, when your husband yells at you for something upsetting him, why do you feel mistreated, unloved, and resentful?

   _____

   _____

   _____

   _____

c. How do you handle this mistreatment and resentment?

_____

_____

_____

_____

Reasons Not to Forgive

2. We know what it feels like to struggle to forgive each other. Read the list of "reasons" not to forgive on pages 119–120 in the book.

   a. From this list, which do you use? Which reason do you use the most often?

   _____

   _____

   _____

   _____

   b. Before going further in this session, take time to ask the Lord to soften your heart, making it open and receptive to what He lovingly will show you about forgiveness. Ask God to make clear to you how to forgive when your spouse wrongs you.

       Requirement: Do not discuss Question 2. Answer the question with self-examination and prayer. If you struggle with forgiveness, do not share this information. You might say things in good faith about your mate's wrongdoing but end up shaming and provoking him or her. Talk only to God. As a group exercise, lift up this matter to God in silent prayer.

Jesus and Paul on Forgiveness

3. Below, read Matthew 18:21–22; Ephesians 4:31–32; and Colossians 3:12–13. Answer the true-and-false questions based on these scriptures.

   Note: Don't spend much time on the true and false. State your opinion and move on to the next question. Do not debate or enter long discussions on "what if."

a. "Then Peter came and said to Him, 'Lord, how often shall my brother sin against me and I forgive him? Up to seven times?' Jesus said to him, 'I do not say to you, up to seven times, but up to seventy times seven'" (Matthew 18:21–22).

Answer the following True or False.

1. Forgiving several times makes you an utter fool. _____

2. Forgiving "seventy times seven" means you become an enabler, keeping this person in sin. _____

3. To forgive from your heart means you must never, ever confront the sin of another person. _____

b. "Let all bitterness and wrath and anger and clamor and slander be put away from you, along with all malice. Be kind to one another, tender-hearted, forgiving each other, just as God in Christ also has forgiven you" (Ephesians 4:31–32).

True or False? Thinking of Christ's forgiveness of us makes forgiveness of our spouse easier. _____

c. "So, as those who have been chosen of God, holy and beloved, put on a heart of compassion, kindness, humility, gentleness and patience; bearing with one another, and forgiving each other, whoever has a complaint against anyone; just as the Lord forgave you, so also should you" (Colossians 3:12–13).

Answer the following True or False.

1. When a person declares, "I will never forgive my mate!" that person sees himself as far more righteous in God's eyes. _____

2. An unforgiving Christ-follower goes to hell. _____

Damned or Disciplined?

4. In the section entitled "Not Loss of Salvation, but Loss of Fellowship," Emerson says, "God will not damn you for your unforgiveness, but He will enact discipline, which He lovingly does for all waywardness." Hebrews 12:5–11 describes God's discipline:

> You have forgotten the exhortation which is addressed to you as sons, "MY SON, DO NOT REGARD LIGHTLY THE DISCIPLINE OF THE LORD, NOR FAINT WHEN YOU ARE REPROVED BY HIM; FOR THOSE WHOM THE LORD LOVES HE DISCIPLINES, AND HE SCOURGES EVERY SON WHOM HE RECEIVES." It is for discipline that you endure; God deals with you as with sons; for what son is there whom his father does not discipline? But if you are without discipline, of which all have become partakers, then you are illegitimate children and not sons. Furthermore, we had earthly fathers to discipline us, and we respected them; shall we not much rather be subject to the Father of spirits, and live? For they disciplined us for a short time as seemed best to them, but He disciplines us for our good, so that we may share His holiness. All discipline for the moment seems not to be joyful, but sorrowful; yet to those who have been trained by it, afterwards it yields the peaceful fruit of righteousness.

a. After reading the Hebrews passage, do you agree that God disciplines you for your sin, including an unforgiving spirit?

_____

_____

_____

b. Does God discipline you for your good so you can experience holiness and peace? What does this mean to you?

_____

_____

_____

c. When a believer refuses to forgive, which of the following happens as evidence of God's discipline?

   1. There is no sense of peace and joy deep in the heart.
   2. There is no confidence when praying and worshiping since the conscience is unclean.

3. There is no meaningful reading of Scripture or application of God's Word.

4. There is no authentic fellowship with other believers.

5. There is no power when ministering to others nor wish to minister to others.

6. There is no boldness in challenging others to be forgiving.

7. There is no moral authority over our children when they observe our un-Christlikeness.

d.   In light of these consequences, why hang on to unforgiveness?

_____

_____

_____

Jesus the Model

5. As a person prepares to forgive, Jesus becomes the model to follow. Wronged more than anyone, even to the point of innocently suffering for the sins of the world, He forgives!

a.   Read the following Scripture passages and express in your own words the primary message of each:

Matthew 11:28–29: "Come to Me, all who are weary and heavy-laden, and I will give you rest. Take My yoke upon you and learn from Me."

_____

_____

_____

_____

1 Peter 2:21: "Christ also suffered for you, leaving you an example for you to follow in His steps."

_____

_____

_____

_____

1 John 2:6: "The one who says he abides in Him ought himself to walk in the same manner as He walked."

_____

_____

_____

_____

    b.   Rate your willingness to imitate Jesus in forgiving others.

Very Willing   Hesitant   Unwilling

The Way Jesus Forgave

6. As our perfect role model, Jesus gives us the secret to forgiveness.

Jesus **sympathized** with the offender.
He **relinquished** the offense to His heavenly Father.
He **anticipated** the Father's help.

These may sound impossible to do, especially if besieged by hurt, but God offers help!

    a.   Which of the three have you done?

_____

_____

    b.   Which of the three do you find the most challenging?

_____

_____

Jesus Sympathized

7. Jesus sympathized to forgive.

Emerson writes, "While He is suffering in horrible agony on the cross, He prays, 'Father, forgive them; for they do not know what they are doing' (Luke 23:34). Jesus prays for forgiveness of the Jews and the Roman soldiers who are taking part in crucifying Him. He forgives by looking beyond their heinous crime to see the ignorance, mindless fear, and blind hatred that have driven them to do this. On the cross, in terrible pain, Jesus sees the true condition of His enemies and feels compassion for them" (pp. 124–125).

a. Jesus prayed on the cross, "Father, forgive them; for they do not know what they are doing." How does this prayer show that Jesus forgave by looking beyond the transgression into the souls of those hurting Him?

_____

_____

_____

_____

b. Read Hebrews 4:15. Why does Jesus sympathize with you? Have you considered that He forgives you because He understands your plight, weaknesses, and ignorance?

_____

_____

_____

_____

c. Do you treat your spouse like Jesus treats you?

_____

_____

_____

_____

Husbands: When your wife reacts in disrespectful ways, does she fully grasp how this hurts you? If not, will you sympathize with her and forgive her? After all, do you react in unloving ways, not realizing how this hurts her?

_____

_____

_____

Wives: When your husband reacts in unloving ways, does he discern how this hurts you? If not, will you sympathize with him and forgive him? After all, do you react in disrespectful ways, not realizing how this hurts him?

_____

_____

_____

d. Generally speaking, would you agree that men and women handle hurt differently? For example, though a husband complains less about personal hurt, does he show his hurt through his anger and silence, and this feels so painful to his wife that she floods with doubt about his love? On the other hand, does a wife talk openly about her hurt not only to her husband but to others, doing so with words sounding so critical that her husband floods with doubt about her respect? If you are guilty, what change must you make?

_____

_____

_____

_____

Looking Beyond

8. Read "When Offended by Your Spouse, SYMPATHIZE" on pages 124–127. When you sympathize, you try to look beyond the offense to other factors that help explain why your spouse offended you.

a. Based on what Emerson writes below, what might help you sympathize with your spouse?

I am often asked, "What if my spouse has hurt me far more than I have hurt my spouse? How can I forgive when I have been treated so unfairly?" Suppose, for example, your husband hurts you with anger and harshness. But you learn that while growing up, your husband's dad wounded him with rage and violence. Consequently, your husband struggles with a serious temper. As you look beyond how he treats you, looking at his upbringing, does this help you forgive? This does not minimize your husband's sin, nor does "looking beyond" suggest you never confront his anger and harshness. But in knowing his background, you see a bigger picture. You empathize. By analogy, suppose your husband mistreats your son. Years later, when your son marries, he carries in his soul an anger problem. Though he controls his anger better than his dad, his anger exceeds that of his father-in-law. How do you want your daughter-in-law to interpret your son? Do you want her to see his great strides or judge him despicable because he falls short of her dad?

_____

_____

_____

_____

b. Read the following story about Emerson and his mom. How does it affect you?

My own mother was an incredible example of one who could look beyond the offense and see other factors. When I was around ten years old, I told my mother how hurt and angry I was because of my father's neglect and cursing at me. She explained, "Well, your dad did not have a dad. His dad died when he was three months old. He doesn't know how to be a daddy." At first I didn't understand, but later I realized my mother was sympathizing with my father even though she hurt far worse for me. Mom was wise, and her attitude enabled her—and me—not to become bitter. Eventually I was able to see my father not as my enemy, but as the victim of an enemy—the death of his own father and the suffering he went through growing up without a dad to love and guide him. I was also able to accept certain things about my father that otherwise would have embarrassed and infuriated me. Yes, his name-calling and outbursts of anger wounded me, but with my mother's guidance I was able to look beyond the offenses to see other factors that explained why he hurt me. Because I was able to understand my father, I was able to forgive him. Looking beyond my father's offenses prevented me from reducing him to a one-sentence description such as "He was a miserable excuse for a father." Years later, when I was in college, my father placed his faith in Jesus Christ. How sad it would have been for me if I had passed judgment on my father in a way the Lord Himself did not. Because the Lord called my dad to Himself, He clearly had not given up on my dad. Because my dad responded, his own heart was obviously tender and open to the Lord. So, what if I had refused to see the painful backdrop of my dad's life? What if I had judged my father as despicable and hopeless, refusing to ever talk to him again? My lack of sympathy and forgiveness would have deprived me of many years of an enjoyable friendship with my dad before he died (pp. 125–126).

My thoughts on this story:

_____

_____

_____

_____

   c.   Those of you who have forgiven by sympathizing with another, tell your group what happened. Talk discreetly but let the others know the power of what took place.

_____

_____

_____

_____

What about Sin?

9. The better you understand your spouse, the more easily you can forgive. But note that sympathizing does NOT mean lowering the standard on sin, or that we do not confront the sin. Emerson gives the example of his own father's harshness and neglect to illustrate this principle. Reread "My Own Father Appeared to Have Evil Will" on page 78, especially the last two paragraphs, which stress that his mother never minimized the seriousness of his father's actions.

   Do not call sin something except what it is. You don't forgive by denying the ugliness of the sin. Peter, for example, never intended to diminish sin's seriousness when writing, "Love covers a multitude of sins" (1 Peter 4:8). Love covers sin but does not redefine sin. Sin is still sin. When Paul says love "does not take into account a wrong suffered" (1 Corinthians 13:5), he acknowledges wrong and the reality of the suffering. However, one forgives by not taking into account the wrong suffered.

      a.   Do you understand that forgiveness does not minimize another's sin? What questions remain?

_____

_____

_____

_____

b. How did Emerson's mother reconcile these two seemingly irreconcilable issues: to sympathize with Emerson's father yet not lower the bar on the wickedness of sin?

_____

_____

_____

_____

c. How might you apply this to your situation? Write what you honestly think.

_____

_____

_____

_____

Self-Righteous Judgment

10. Jesus shows that judging ends when looking at the log in your eye and not at the speck in your spouse's eye. Forgiveness becomes easier when you stop throwing stones as a self-righteous, sinless person.

Matthew 7:1–3 says, "Do not judge so that you will not be judged. For in the way you judge, you will be judged; and by your standard of measure, it will be measured to you. Why do you look at the speck that is in your brother's eye, but do not notice the log that is in your own eye?"

_____

_____

_____

_____

a. Why is self-righteousness the greatest enemy of forgiveness?

_____

_____

_____

_____

b. What does the Lord feel when He forgives us of our sins toward our spouse, yet
    we do not forgive our spouse of his or her sins against us?

    _____

    _____

    _____

    _____

c. On page 127, read the examples of a husband and a wife who struggled to forgive
    perhaps the toughest offense—adultery. Write out the process they each went
    through to find it in their hearts to forgive their spouses.

    _____

    _____

    _____

    _____

Jesus Relinquished

11. Read "As You Work Toward Forgiveness, RELINQUISH the Offense to Your
    Heavenly Father" on pages 128–130.

    a. Why is it possible to be resentful even after you sympathize with your spouse?

        _____

        _____

        _____

        _____

    b. The next step toward forgiveness is to relinquish your will to God and surrender
        to Him whatever you have against your spouse. Let's look again at our Perfect
        Role Model, Jesus, to see how He relinquished His will to the Father. Read the
        following verses and briefly state what Jesus did to relinquish.

        In Luke 22:42 Jesus says, "Father, if You are willing, remove this cup from Me;
        yet not My will, but Yours be done."

        1 Peter 2:21–23: For you have been called for this purpose, since Christ also
        suffered for you, leaving you an example for you to follow in His steps, WHO

COMMITTED NO SIN, NOR WAS ANY DECEIT FOUND IN HIS
MOUTH; and while being reviled, He did not revile in return; while suffering,
He uttered no threats, but kept entrusting Himself to Him who judges
righteously.

_____

_____

_____

_____

c. Since Jesus surrendered His sinless will to the perfect will of His Father, why is it
in your best interest to pray, "Not my will, but Yours be done"? Why do some
hang on to self-will, choosing to retaliate with deceit, reviling, and threatening?
Have you?

_____

_____

_____

_____

d. If you have not relinquished your determination to punish your spouse, pray this
prayer right now: "Father, not my will of bitterness and retaliation, but Your will
of forgiveness be done."

_____

_____

_____

_____

Stop the Bitterness

12. In Ephesians 4:31 Paul tells all believers to "let all bitterness and wrath and anger and
clamor and slander be put away from you, along with all malice."

From his years of ministry, Emerson concluded that people have far more control
over their emotions than he originally thought. What do you think of his following
statements? "God does help you forgive when you feel helpless to forgive, but other
times He shows to you the need to put away bitterness. . . . We can get rid of
bitterness—if we want to. I have seen that the ultimate reason many people are bitter
is that they want to be bitter."

a.   In what ways can you identify with these statements?

_____

_____

_____

_____

b.   Do you find yourself holding on to bitterness as an old friend? God's Word teaches us that you can relinquish the bitterness, wrath, anger, and malice. If you need to, pray this again: "Father, not my will of bitterness and retaliation, but Your will of forgiveness be done."

Jesus Anticipated

13. We have already acknowledged that forgiveness is next to impossible without Christ. To grasp fully this reality, read "The Final Step Toward Forgiveness: ANTICIPATE" on pages 130–134.

Anticipate means having hope or trust that God will work. When Jesus prayed, "Thy will be done," He believed the will of His Father would be accomplished. This is why "he entrusted himself to him who judges justly" (1 Peter 2:23 NIV). In other words, after you relinquish, anticipate! You need to foresee God entering your world. As you entrust yourself to God, anticipate His working on your behalf.

A wife writes: "A friend was specifically praying that I would be willing to do whatever God wanted me to do. After tremendous conviction and a broken, humbled spirit, I knew I had to write Blake a letter apologizing to him, not only for not respecting him like I should have, but also apologizing for not handling my anger in godly ways. I also included some other things, such as telling him some things I appreciated about him. Until that day, I didn't even realize how angry I was. After I wrote the letter, I felt like a heavy load had been lifted, and I had tremendous peace. It was the most supernatural thing I had ever experienced. I had no idea what was going to happen from there, but I just acted out of obedience, and it has been amazing how God has blessed me and also brought some healing to our marriage" (pp. 131–132).

a. She speaks clearly: "It was the most supernatural thing I had ever experienced." Have you met God like this? Describe what the Lord did.

_____

_____

_____

_____

b. When looking to God in anticipation, why is forgiving a spouse made easier?

_____

_____

_____

_____

Better Communication

14. Not only will some of you experience God's powerful presence, your forgiveness is bound to help your marital communication. All three of these steps (sympathy, relinquishment, and anticipation) build better communication with your mate.

    If you have **sympathized**, you will talk to your mate with understanding rather than making your case about your hurts. (Remember, mutual understanding is the key to good communication.)

    If you have **relinquished** your resentment, your spouse will detect a different tone and attitude in your words and will talk to you with a better attitude. (Remember, bitterness shuts down your spouse. When bitterness leaves, your spouse will open up to you more.)

    To **anticipate** is to hope in God. When your expectations center on what God will do, you get rid of unrealistic expectations of your spouse. (Remember, when you place your deepest confidence in God, you remove unrealistic expectations and pressure from your spouse and come across friendlier, which enhances communication.)

a. Which of these three steps do you need to work on the most?

_____

_____

_____

_____

b. If you have experienced improvement in your communication from these three steps, write a few sentences about what happened. If in a group, share your success with them.

_____

_____

_____

_____

PART FOUR: THE ENERGIZING CYCLE: TO BETTER COMMUNICATE, MEET YOUR SPOUSE'S NEEDS

SESSION SIX

⟶⟶⟵⟵

In this session, we start Part IV, The Energizing Cycle: To Better Communicate, Meet Your Spouse's Needs. Because you have figured out how to stop the Crazy Cycle, our goal is to help you maintain a happy, communicating relationship by getting on the Energizing Cycle, which says:

HIS LOVE MOTIVATES HER RESPECT.
HER RESPECT MOTIVATES HIS LOVE.

CHAPTER EIGHT: "ENJOY WIN-WIN COMMUNICATION ON THE ENERGIZING CYCLE"

When you stay on the Energizing Cycle, the Crazy Cycle has no chance to spin unless you forget to use the tools at your disposal. We will discuss these tools in the next few sessions. Let's begin by reading Chapter Eight, "Enjoy Win-Win Communication on the Energizing Cycle."

Verbal Flamethrowers

1. Emerson writes, "I want to emphasize that slowing and even stopping the Crazy Cycle doesn't result in automatically experiencing the Energizing Cycle. Putting out the negative doesn't kindle the positive, nor is success merely the absence of failure. What you and your spouse must do is go beyond being reactive . . . and be proactive" (p. 138).

   a. If a spouse stops words that sound contemptuous and hateful (turning off the flamethrowers), does this enrich the marriage?

   _____

   _____

   _____

b. If you heard your spouse make the following comment, what would it do to you?

Your husband says, "I struggle with telling my wife that I love her."

_____

_____

_____

Your wife says, "I find it hard to say to my husband, 'I respect you.'"

_____

_____

_____

Emerson's Two Discoveries

2. After asking himself two questions, Emerson discovered two wonderful insights:

a. Question 1:
    "As I read Ephesians 5:33, I believe God prompted me to ask: 'What would happen if a wife met her husband's need for respect?'"

    What did Emerson discover (p. 139)? Do you agree or disagree with his conclusion?

    _____

    _____

    _____

    _____

b. Question 2:
    "As I pondered that, another question arose: 'What would happen if a husband met his wife's need for love?'"

    What did Emerson find (p. 139)? Do you agree or disagree with his conclusion?

    _____

    _____

    _____

    _____

The Key to Motivation

3. The key to motivating another person is meeting that person's deepest need.

Wives, share why a husband energizes his wife when speaking with words of love.

_____

_____

_____

Husbands, share why a wife energizes her husband when speaking with words of respect.

_____

_____

_____

Defining Love: C-O-U-P-L-E

4. Emerson spells love to a wife as: Closeness, Openness, Understanding, Peacemaking, Loyalty, and Esteem. C-O-U-P-L-E paints a picture of the wife's inner world. Her thoughts and feelings revolve around C-O-U-P-L-E. She thinks pink, and when her husband speaks the language of pink—remaining a man of honor, never becoming effeminate—his wife feels loved. His wife feels energized and motivated!

a. Which statement below defines Closeness, Openness, Understanding, Peacemaking, Loyalty, and Esteem? Place the letter (C-O-U-P-L-E) in front of the definition.

_____ A loving husband is to assure his wife of his love and commitment, making her feel secure in the covenant they have together because she knows he would never "deal treacherously" with her.

_____ A loving husband is to live with his wife in an empathetic way, willing to listen when she is concerned or has a problem instead of trying to fix her. As he listens, he lets her know he is interested by paying attention and giving appropriate feedback.

_____ A loving husband is to be kind and gentle, opening up to his wife, sharing his thoughts and ideas, instead of closing off his spirit by acting preoccupied or disinterested, or by being secretly mad or embittered.

_____ A loving husband is willing to say, "Honey, I'm sorry. Please forgive me" because he knows that he and his wife are to no longer be two, but one, living in peace and harmony.

_____ A loving husband honors and cherishes his wife in specific ways, making her feel she is first in his heart and honored as a "fellow heir of the grace of life."

_____ A loving husband is to cleave to his wife, taking time to talk, being affectionate, close to her heart—and not just when he wants sex.

b. Wives, which of these do you feel your husband does best? As a result, do you feel more loved and energized?

_____

_____

c. Husbands, which of these definitions have you least understood? Are you willing to work on this area as a way to energize your wife?

_____

_____

Biblical Basis for C-O-U-P-L-E

5. **Husbands:** The acronym C-O-U-P-L-E spells six ways husbands can love their wives. Derived from Scripture, these principles explain how to love a wife. A husband energizes his wife when he follows these truths. Beside each letter below, look up the scriptures that contain a command to husbands or a truth about a wife's feminine nature, and write the key biblical idea(s) next to the verse.

C – Closeness (Genesis 2:24): For example, the biblical idea is "cleave."

_____

_____

O – Openness (Colossians 3:19):

_____

_____

U – Understanding (1 Peter 3:7a):

_____

_____

P – Peacemaking (Matthew 19:6):

_____

_____

L – Loyalty (Malachi 2:14–15):

_____

_____

E – Esteem (1 Peter 3:7b):

_____

_____

Defining Respect: C-H-A-I-R-S

6. Emerson spells respect to a husband: Conquest, Hierarchy, Authority, Insight, Relationship, and Sexuality. C-H-A-I-R-S paints a picture of a husband's inner world. His thoughts and feelings revolve around C-H-A-I-R-S. He thinks blue, and when his wife speaks the language of blue—remaining fully feminine and never becoming masculine—her husband feels respected. Her husband feels energized and motivated!

    a. Which statement below defines Conquest, Hierarchy, Authority, Insight, Relationship, and Sexuality? Place the letter (C-H-A-I-R-S) in front of the definition.

    _____ Because Scripture teaches that a wife should *phileo* her husband (love him as a friend), the respectful wife is called to appreciate his desire for shoulder-to-shoulder companionship, realizing that she is to be her husband's friend as well as his lover.

    _____ Because Scripture makes the husband responsible for loving and caring for his wife, she is called to respect his leadership, not being contentious and combative, but appreciating his desire to serve and lead her and the family as she supports, and never undermines, his position.

_____ Because Scripture states the husband is the head of his wife as Christ is head of the church, the respectful wife is called to submit to her husband by appreciating his desire to protect and provide for her and the family, thanking him for his efforts.

_____ Because Scripture indicates that a woman can be tricked by cunning voices of the culture and led astray by carnal intuitions, the respectful wife is called to appreciate her husband's desire to analyze and counsel, always listening carefully to what he has to say to guard or guide her. If she disagrees with his ideas, she differs with him respectfully.

_____ Because she understands that her husband needs her sexually, the respectful wife does not deprive him, but appreciates his desire for sexual intimacy, knowing that sex is symbolic of his deeper need for respect (Song of Solomon 4:1–15).

_____ Because God made man to work, the respectful wife is called to appreciate his desire to do a good job and achieve in his field of endeavor. She does this by thanking him for his efforts and letting him know she is behind him (Genesis 2:18).

b. Husbands, which of these do you feel your wife does best? As a result, do you feel more respected and energized?

_____

_____

c. Wives, which of these definitions have you least understood? Are you willing to work on this area as a way to energize your husband?

_____

_____

Biblical Basis for C-H-A-I-R-S

7. **Wives:** The acronym C-H-A-I-R-S spells six ways wives can respect their husbands. Derived from Scripture, these principles explain how to respect a husband. A wife energizes her husband when she follows these truths. Beside each letter below, look up the scriptures that contain a command to wives or a truth about a husband's masculine nature, and write the key idea(s) next to the verse.

C – Conquest (Genesis 2:15): For example, the biblical idea is that the man, Adam, was to "cultivate" and "keep" the "garden."

_____

_____

H – Hierarchy (Ephesians 5:22–25):

_____

_____

A – Authority (Proverbs 21:9; Ephesians 5:22; 1 Timothy 2:12):

_____

_____

I – Insight (2 Corinthians 11:3; 1 Timothy 2:14):

_____

_____

R – Relationship (Song of Solomon 5:16; Titus 2:4):

_____

_____

S – Sexuality (Proverbs 5:19; 1 Corinthians 7:5):

_____

_____

"If-Then" Principle

8. One of the exciting results of applying the principles in C-O-U-P-L-E and C-H-A-I-R-S is the "if-then" principle. Read pages 145–154 to review.

Emerson writes, "As we have seen, the Energizing Cycle is based on the Love and Respect Connection, which operates according to the "if-then" rule: if she does something respectful, then he is likely to do something loving; if he does something loving, then she is likely to do something respectful. . . . I like to describe the Energizing Cycle by saying the principles in one acronym cross-pollinate the principles in the other acronym. Cross-pollination, as you know, is the process that causes plants to be fruitful and productive. And that's exactly what C-O-U-P-L-E and C-H-A-I-R-S will do for your marriage. Just about any set of combinations will work."

a. When both the husband and wife apply the "if-then" principle, they experience the Energizing Cycle. Do you agree or disagree? Why?

_____

_____

_____

_____

b. How much do you apply the cross-pollination of C-O-U-P-L-E and C-H-A-I-R-S, which puts you on the Energizing Cycle? Circle the number that best describes you.

1. I do not apply the "if-then" principle of C-O-U-P-L-E and C-H-A-I-R-S. I need to pay attention to this section.

2. I apply the "if-then" principle of C-O-U-P-L-E and C-H-A-I-R-S a little. I need to pay more attention to this section.

3. I apply the "if-then" principle of C-O-U-P-L-E and C-H-A-I-R-S pretty well. Still, I need to guard against letting down. I need to pay attention to this section.

Cross-Pollination

9. Consider how well you do with the cross-pollination of C-O-U-P-L-E and C-H-A-I-R-S.

a. Of the following combinations below, which do you see working best in your marriage? Circle once. Which combination needs the most work? Circle twice.

How CLOSENESS connects with RELATIONSHIP

When a husband chooses to be close and talk face-to-face with his wife, then his wife is motivated to be in shoulder-to-shoulder relationship with him without talking.

Conversely, if a wife chooses to be in a shoulder-to-shoulder relationship with her husband *sans* talking, then her husband is motivated to be close and talk face-to-face with her.

How OPENNESS connects with SEXUALITY

If a husband chooses to be open, heart-to-heart with his wife, then she is motivated to be open to him sexually.

And of course the reverse is true. If she is sexual with him, he will be willing to open up to her.

How UNDERSTANDING connects with INSIGHT

If a husband chooses to listen to his wife's concerns and problems in an understanding way, then she will be motivated to appreciate his insights.

And as a wife listens to her husband's insights, views, and opinions, he will be motivated to listen to her with understanding instead of immediately trying to fix her problem.

How PEACEMAKING connects with AUTHORITY

If a husband chooses to be a peacemaker, taking the needs and concerns of his wife totally into account during any kind of argument or conflict, his wife will be motivated in turn to respond to his authority during stalemates.

By the same token, if a wife chooses to respect her husband's authority (desire to serve and lead), he will be motivated to make peace with her and try to meet her needs and concerns during conflict at any level.

How LOYALTY connects to CONQUEST

If a husband chooses to be loyal to his wife and family and constantly lets her know it, she is motivated to be supportive of his career conquests outside the family.

And when a wife backs her husband in his desire to work and achieve in his field of endeavor, it motivates and encourages him to remain loyal to her and the rest of the family.

How ESTEEM connects to HIERARCHY

If a husband chooses to esteem or honor his wife and her role in the family, then his wife is motivated to accept and respect his role as head of the family hierarchy and his desire to protect and provide for her and their children.

When a wife is content with her husband as the head who protects and provides for the family, he is motivated to esteem, honor, and respect her by treasuring her as first in importance to him.

b.   As a mature person, working on your "half" of the combination, think of a way you can apply this principle in your marriage. Make a commitment to focus on the application this week. Use this space to write your thoughts.

_____

_____

_____

_____

Twin Vending Machines?

10. With every great idea misinterpretation and misuse occur. How might the "if-then" principle backfire if you focus solely on self-serving outcomes? (Read the sections "C-O-U-P-L-E and C-H-A-I-R-S Are Not Twin Vending Machines" and "The Energizing Cycle Has Long-Term Potential" on pages 157–160 for more insight.)

a.   Agree or Disagree? When a husband does something in C-O-U-P-L-E, he has a right to expect his wife to do something in C-H-A-I-R-S, and vice versa.

b.   Briefly state why these comments backfire:

1. A husband comments, "Look, I was verbally open with you. When can we have sex?"

_____

_____

_____

2. A wife comments, "Look, I was with you shoulder to shoulder, saying nothing. When can we talk face-to-face and really work on the relationship?"

_____

_____

_____

3. A husband comments, "Look, I listened to your points about this decision. Now, you are supposed to submit to my desire to borrow money. You must co-sign."

_____

_____

_____

4. A wife comments, "Look, I know you are the head. But you must make decisions in keeping with what I want and know to be right."

_____

_____

_____

The Unconditional

11. Though the Energizing Cycle opens communication in marriage, Emerson cautions you to remember that all-important word: *unconditional.*

   a. Why must a husband commit to speak lovingly when a wife does not respond with respectful words?

   _____

   _____

   _____

   b. Why must a wife commit to speak respectfully when a husband does not respond with loving words?

   _____

   _____

   _____

Acknowledge Goodwill

12. Though neither of you completely meets the other's expectations, you can remind one another that you have goodwill.

    a. A wife writes, "Now we know what the Crazy Cycle is like. We can pinpoint right when we are getting on it, and we now have the tools to fix it immediately. I say, 'Babe, can you try to tell me that in pink, I am not sure if I understand you correctly.' Or something like that, in just a regular conversation. It is really fun. People might think we are crazy with the whole pink and blue thing, but it really works!! It makes the really, really complicated thing (men and women communicating) really, really simple."

    Though this husband appears insensitive, how does this wife send the message to her husband that she believes he has good intentions?

    _____

    _____

    _____

    _____

    This week, how will you let your spouse know that you believe s/he has goodwill?

    _____

    _____

    _____

    _____

    b. Have you ever voiced to your mate that you have goodwill, perhaps on the heels of failing to be respectful or loving? How might you reassure your spouse of your goodwill this week? Jot your ideas below.

    _____

    _____

    _____

    _____

SESSION SEVEN

———

In preparation for this session, please read Chapter Nine, "Decode—and Then Use C-H-A-I-R-S to Energize Him" and Chapter Ten, "Decode—and Then Use C-O-U-P-L-E to Energize Her."

Though the principles of C-H-A-I-R-S and C-O-U-P-L-E successfully influence marriages, marital communication still requires that you learn to DECODE. To keep the Energizing Cycle going strong, you can't get too good at decoding. In this session we will learn more about the skillful art of decoding our mates.

CHAPTER NINE: "DECODE—AND THEN USE C-H-A-I-R-S TO ENERGIZE HIM"

Note to Husbands: The questions in this chapter are for wives but you are invited to read along. See the second half of this session (Chapter Ten) for your assignment.

Three Hours of Sitting

1. Read the story about Emerson's frustrating day on pages 161–167. Let's dissect this story by evaluating it through the lens of Love and Respect.

    a. While waiting, waiting, and waiting at the doctor's office, why did Emerson feel disrespected?

    _____

    _____

    _____

b. When Emerson e-mailed Sarah about his frustration and later interrupted her time with her girlfriend, how did he send a coded message to Sarah about feeling disrespected?

_____

_____

_____

c. How did his reaction to what happened at the doctor's office threaten to put him and Sarah on the Crazy Cycle? What did he want from Sarah when he vented to her?

_____

_____

_____

d. Did Sarah decode his message, or did she take the bait?

_____

_____

_____

e. Although Sarah felt some anger at first, did she take it personally and react over the unfair treatment, or did she exercise self-control? Later, how did she resolve her feelings of anger?

_____

_____

_____

Emerson summarizes this story with the following wisdom: "Whatever offensive words might have been spoken, always listen for your spouse's basic need. At the very bottom of things, in every case and in every conversation, you can do your marriage a huge favor by assuming she is seeking to feel loved or, in the case of this chapter, he is seeking to feel respected—and then give your spouse some grace!"

The Male's God-Given Desires

2. In the section entitled "How to Use C-H-A-I-R-S to Decode Your Husband's Cries for Respect" (pp. 168–169), you see six biblical truths (C-H-A-I-R-S) pointing to the male's need for respect. Each concept is a revelation from God about the spirit of the male. In fact, each biblical passage in C-H-A-I-R-S shows us an important desire in the male. For example, that God called Adam to work ("C"), as He calls all men to work, tells us that God put a desire in Adam to work. Your husband has this desire to

work. When you value his desire to work, your husband feels respected! In like manner, as a wife, C-O-U-P-L-E points to your female need for love. These six biblical passages (C-O-U-P-L-E) reveal truth about your female desires. You desire Closeness, Openness, Understanding, Peacemaking, Loyalty, and Esteem. When a man values these desires in you, you feel loved!

a. Does this teaching about a husband's six desires help you appreciate the C-H-A-I-R-S principles and God's design of men? Why or why not?

_____

_____

_____

_____

b. Why is it important to show respect for your husband's *desires that lie beneath* C-H-A-I-R-S rather than his *performance* of C-H-A-I-R-S? For example, a husband desires to work but he might lack success at work. Can you show respect for his desire to work though neither of you approve of his performance?

_____

_____

_____

_____

c. Of the six concepts in C-H-A-I-R-S, which concept needs the most attention in your marriage? If you do not know, ask your husband. Focus on this category, answer the questions, and do the applications. Acquaint yourself with the other five concepts but place most of your energy in this one area over the next several weeks. Then give attention to another concept. This approach prevents you from feeling overwhelmed.

_____

_____

_____

_____

C – CONQUEST

3. If he feels his work is unappreciated, you'll hear about it. Because "God took the man and put him into the Garden of Eden to cultivate it and keep it" (Genesis 2:15), wives need to grasp why and how men feel compelled to work. But because so many

women have full-time careers outside the home, they can overlook the man's God-given desire to work and succeed (conquer) in his field.

a. Ask yourself: Does my husband know I have high regard for his desire to work? Do I realize that my recognition of the significance of my husband's work energizes him? Do I know that he has fond feelings of affection for me when I honor this desire?

_____

_____

_____

b. Genesis 2:18 says, "Then the LORD God said, 'It is not good for the man to be alone; I will make him a helper suitable for him.'" What does this verse mean to you? How do you think a "helper" can help a husband feel respected?

_____

_____

_____

c. For the busy career woman, or the mom wrestling with raising the children and keeping the home running, there may be little interest to wear the hat called "husband's helper." Such a woman might ask, "But what about ME? Who's MY helper?" Have you ever felt this way? If so, how might you reconcile these feelings with God creating you as a "helper suitable"?

_____

_____

_____

d. From page 170, write out the statement here that best expresses your appreciation for his desire to work (conquest) and share the statement with him. For example, "Let's set aside some time tonight just for us. I want to hear about what's happening at work."

Note: Writing or speaking this to your husband may seem awkward, silly, and trivial, but this exercise can do three things. One, it requires you to think about "respect talk," which is foreign to many wives. Two, when sincerely expressed it energizes your husband. And three, you show your obedience to God as you apply Ephesians 5:33.

_____

_____

_____

e. Going Deeper (*Optional*): For a complete discussion of Conquest, see Chapter Sixteen in *Love & Respect* (Nashville: Integrity, 2004).

H – HIERARCHY

4. If you do not value his desire to protect and provide, he may send a coded message. Because God calls him to be "the head of the wife, as Christ also is the head of the church" (Ephesians 5:23), your husband needs to hear your gratitude for his desire and duty to protect you and to provide and even die for you.

a. Words like *headship* appear loaded to women influenced by feminism. How do you react to the terms *hierarchy* and *head of his wife*?

_____

_____

_____

b. Can you think of a time when you devalued or criticized your husband's desire to protect and provide? Describe what happened.

_____

_____

_____

c. Ask yourself: Do I express my respect and appreciation for my husband's sense of responsibility for me, or do I rail against the biblical idea of the husband's headship, feeling that my husband views headship as a right *over* me, not a responsibility *for* me?

_____

_____

_____

d. Do I understand how a statement of respect for his commitment to protect me touches him? Write a statement to your husband expressing appreciation for his desire to protect and provide. (Refer to the examples on pages 171–172 for ideas.)

_____

_____

_____

e. Going Deeper (*Optional*): Emerson has done an in-depth study of biblical hierarchy. If you would like to know more about his belief that male chauvinism and radical feminism misinterpret Scripture, see Chapter Seventeen in *Love & Respect*, especially pages 205–209.

A – AUTHORITY

5. Pay attention to and respect his desire to serve and to lead. Because Scripture commands the husband to responsibly care for his wife and family, God calls the wife to respect the husband's authority to carry out this responsibility. A contentious and combative attitude fails to appreciate a man's desire to serve and lead the family. God expects her to support and never sabotage this authority (Proverbs 21:9; Ephesians 5:22).

a. Ask yourself: Do I let my husband know that, because he has the responsibility to protect and provide for me, I recognize he has primary authority in our family? Said another way, am I on record with my husband that, because he has 51 percent of the responsibility (to die for me!), he has 51 percent of the authority? Or, do I hypocritically insist on an "egalitarian" marriage with equal authority, yet I contradict egalitarianism by expecting him to bear the primary responsibility?

_____

_____

_____

b. Think of a time when you got on the Crazy Cycle because you said, "You can't do that—we're equal!" As you exercised veto power (meaning you have 51 percent of the authority and your husband has 51 percent of the responsibility), did you observe your husband's spirit deflate? Did your good ideas deflate him, or was it your disrespectful attitude? How might you communicate your disagreement in a respectful way? Write your thoughts and ideas.

_____

_____

_____

_____

c. Write a statement to your husband about your respect for his desire, given to him by God, to responsibly lead. (Refer to page 173 for ideas on respectful, energizing responses.) Note: Don't assume that because you have not seen this desire that it is missing in your husband. Some husbands desire to lead but have moved into passivity out of fear of the wife's disapproval. Acknowledging this desire encourages him to risk acting on this God-given desire.

_____

_____

_____

_____

    d. Going Deeper (*Optional*): For a complete explanation of the "51 percent rule" and other aspects of Authority, see Chapter Eighteen of *Love & Respect*, especially pages 221–22.

I – INSIGHT

6. Don't let your woman's intuition deafen you to his desire to analyze and counsel. Women have received credit over the years for "women's intuition" and rightly so. However, we cannot ignore scriptures such as 1 Timothy 2:14 and 2 Corinthians 11:3, which remind us that cunning voices and carnal intuitions trick and deceive some women. As Emerson says, "Feminists might call these passages 'a chauvinist put-down' but there is wisdom here for the wife who will see it."

    a. What are your thoughts on the above statements? How do Genesis 3:17; 2 Corinthians 11:3; and 1 Timothy 2:14 caution wives on this matter?

_____

_____

_____

_____

    b. Have you felt your husband is trying to "fix you" with his advice? If so, how does this teaching on a man's desire to analyze and counsel change your perspective?

_____

_____

_____

_____

c. Ask yourself: Do I realize that my husband and I are a team—that our marriage needs my intuition and his insight? If my husband offers ideas or opinions contrary to mine, do I welcome his perspective even though I disagree?

_____

_____

_____

_____

When I differ with his ideas, do I differ respectfully or with condescension?

_____

_____

_____

_____

d. Write your husband a note that expresses respect for his desire to share his insight and counsel with you (refer to the list on pages 174–75 for help).

_____

_____

_____

_____

R – RELATIONSHIP

7. His desire for shoulder-to-shoulder friendship may seem a bit odd, but keep your ears open for it anyway. When Paul gives advice to the older women to teach the younger women "to love their husbands and children" (Titus 2:4 NIV), he uses the Greek word *phileo*, which means to love him as a friend. This idea repeats itself in Song of Solomon 5:16.

a. What are your thoughts on Emerson's statement, "Being friendly to her man is one of the most effective things a woman can do to strengthen her marriage"?

_____

_____

_____

b. Does your husband think that you like him? Circle the answer that best represents you and tell why.

Yes, he knows I do   It depends on the day   Probably not

c. How does your level of "friendship" compare to the level of friendship the two of you shared while dating? Circle your answer.

Better   About the same   We are no longer friends

d. List three ways to be friendly to your husband and act on one of them this week. Remember the shoulder-to-shoulder activity!

_____

_____

_____

S – SEXUALITY

8. Your husband's desire for sexual intimacy runs deeper than merely physical. At the Love and Respect conferences, Emerson's wife, Sarah, speaks to the women about sexuality. She challenges wives to grapple with how they would feel if their husbands did not talk to them for a week, a month, or even years. If this happened to you, would you feel loved by your husband? Obviously not. This would devastate you. In the same way, a husband feels saddened and disrespected when his wife refuses to meet his sexual need for weeks, months, or even years. Unfortunately, too many people miss the husband's underlying pain and focus on his supposed lust and the wife's disgust.

a. Share your thoughts about the idea that your husband needs sexual release just as you need emotional release (intimacy).

_____

_____

_____

_____

b.   How strongly do you agree or disagree with the idea that sex conveys respect to a husband?

_____

_____

_____

_____

c.   From eternity past, God made a blueprint for human sexuality. His design remains precious and pure to Him. Therefore, can a wife trust God when reading 1 Corinthians 7:5? Will she stop depriving her husband because she believes in God's blueprint for sex?

_____

_____

_____

_____

This includes the husband. Will he trust God as he seeks to meet his wife's sexual needs? A growing number of husbands deprive their wives. The Bible instructs both to serve the other's sexual needs (1 Corinthians 7:2–4). Jot down your thoughts on what it means for a couple to operate according to God's design for sex, out of love and obedience to Jesus Christ.

_____

_____

_____

_____

Under this category of "Sexuality" in the context of C-H-A-I-R-S, do you think a wife can find delight in doing God's will by meeting her husband's needs? How would you counsel a wife to see the holiness of God's design for sex, especially if she possesses fears from her past?

_____

_____

_____

_____

d. Write a statement here that expresses your wish to honor your husband's sexuality. For ideas, read the statements on pages 177–78. Will you open up the topic of sexuality with your husband this week by sharing with him what you wrote?

_____

_____

_____

_____

Teachability

9. All the decoding in the world won't help your marriage if you don't allow it to shape your behavior.

a. Back in Session One, you read C-H-A-I-R-S: A Checkup for Wives. In question 6 of your assignment in that session, you were asked to do an honest self-assessment on how you were showing respect to your husband, based on the C-H-A-I-R-S principles. After digging into these principles this week, what grade would you give yourself?

_____

_____

b. For the Risk Taker! Ask your husband what grade he gave you. Pray for an open heart to hear your husband's "insight" on how you are doing. Choose the area you need the most work on, and humbly ask the Lord to help you improve. Write the steps you plan to take in the space provided, along with a specific day or time that you plan to apply them.

_____

_____

_____

Note to husbands and wives: In sharing areas of weakness, please treat one another with love and respect. You progress in your marriage as you decode one another's behavior with sensitivity and patience.

CHAPTER TEN: "DECODE—AND THEN USE C-O-U-P-L-E TO ENERGIZE HER"

Note to wives: These questions are written for husbands, but you are invited to read along.

No Singing of "Kum Ba Ya"

1. At the beginning of the chapter, you read about Emerson's inability to decode Sarah's negativity and discouragement during the years their children were teenagers (pages 180–85).

   a. What did Sarah mean when she said, "I'm the one who needs to run away"? What coded message was she sending?

   _____

   _____

   _____

   _____

   b. In the second story, what is lurking behind Sarah's question to Emerson, "Do you not care where your son is?" Did Emerson decode Sarah's words?

   _____

   _____

   _____

   _____

   c. Although Emerson's reactions did not spin them on the Crazy Cycle, neither did he open up communication. As Sarah felt alone and unloved, Emerson felt blamed and inadequate. As a husband, do you identify with Emerson's feelings? Do you see why Sarah felt as she did?

   _____

   _____

   _____

   _____

Six Female Longings

2. When a wife sounds negative, beneath her words is often a cry for reassurance of her husband's love. Meeting this need for love happens by practicing C-O-U-P-L-E:

Closeness, Openness, Understanding, Peacemaking, Loyalty, and Esteem. Using these biblically based principles to decode the negativity keeps you off the Crazy Cycle and on the Energizing Cycle.

a. Read about what Emerson would do differently with the insight he has about love and respect (pp. 183–186). In the space below, jot down a few key concepts Emerson has learned to use to decode Sarah.

_____

_____

_____

_____

b. Of the six concepts in C-O-U-P-L-E, which needs the most attention in your marriage? If you do not know, ask your wife. Focus on this category, answer the questions, and do the applications. Acquaint yourself with the other five concepts, but place most of your energy in this one area over the next several weeks. Then give attention to another concept. This approach prevents you from feeling overwhelmed.

_____

_____

_____

_____

C – CLOSENESS

3. If you're not close, you'll hear about it. A loving husband cleaves to his wife, taking time to talk, being affectionate, close to her heart—and not just when he wants sex (Genesis 2:24).

a. Husbands, when your wife pushes you to talk and comments, "All you ever want me for is sex!" what is in her heart? Do you look past her critical comments and decode her need? Why or why not?

_____

_____

_____

_____

b. Ask yourself: Have I been moving toward my wife or away from her? Do I tell her that I love her, admire her, and appreciate her—or do I save those remarks for when I want sex?

_____

_____

_____

_____

c. Write a statement to your wife expressing your wish for closeness (refer to examples on page 188 for ideas, or write your own). For example, "I changed my work schedule. I want to spend more time together."

Note: Writing or speaking this to your wife may seem awkward, silly, and trivial, but this exercise can do three things. One, it requires you to think about communicating with "love talk." Two, when sincerely expressed, it energizes your wife. And three, you show your obedience to God as you apply Ephesians 5:33.

_____

_____

_____

_____

O – OPENNESS

4. Act distant or irritated and she may think you are mad at her. (She'll feel unloved and certainly won't feel motivated to show respect.) This is why a loving husband is not to close off in anger but be gentle, opening up to his wife, sharing his thoughts and ideas without annoyance and resentment.

In Colossians 3:19, Paul tells a husband to love and not be embittered (closing off in anger). Why? Whatever the wife does to make her husband mad and cause him to withdraw in silence must not be construed as deliberate. To the apostle, she seeks love! Thus, Paul instructs the husband to love. Love meets her need for love and softens her provocative behavior.

a. Emerson points out that several translations of this passage use the word *harsh*. Proverbs 29:22 says, "An angry man stirs up strife" and nowhere is this clearer than in our homes! Can you think of a time when you sent your wife spinning on the Crazy Cycle by acting irritated or speaking harshly to her? Describe what happened.

_____

_____

_____

_____

   b.   Ask yourself: Do I share my thoughts and problems with her (a big part of closeness), or do I keep things to myself to prove I am strong and capable? Do I come across as irritated or angry when she tries to draw me out, or am I open and transparent when she shows concern or curiosity?

   c.   Write a statement to your wife that expresses your willingness to stop closing off in anger (to get respect) and to show gentleness and openness so she'll feel loved. (Refer to examples on page 189 for ideas, or create your own).

_____

_____

_____

_____

U – UNDERSTAND

5. She prefers that you listen, not lecture. A loving husband lives with his wife "in an understanding way" (see 1 Peter 3:7), willing to pay attention to her concerns and problems without trying to fix her.

   a.   Husbands, when your wife says, "You just don't get it!" what is she trying to communicate?

_____

_____

_____

_____

b. Why is "fixing" her so frustrating to her?

_____

_____

_____

_____

c. Ask yourself: When she shares her concerns or problems, do I listen and let her talk, or do I try to solve the problem? Do I understand that talking is as important to my wife as sex is to me?

_____

_____

_____

_____

d. Write a statement to your wife that expresses your desire to understand her. (See page 190 for suggestions, or write your own.)

_____

_____

_____

_____

P – PEACEMAKING

6. When God calls you to become "one" (Matthew 19:6), He calls you to live in peace and harmony with each other (Ephesians 2:14–17). When a wife feels "one" with her husband, she feels loved. A husband need not live perfectly before his wife to experience such peace. Confessing imperfection moves the marriage in the right direction. He need only say, "Honey, I'm sorry. Please forgive me."

a. What is your wife telling you when she asks, "Why must I always say 'I'm sorry' and not you?" Is she communicating disrespect because she wants you to grovel, or is she appealing to you to apologize so she can feel loved?

_____

_____

_____

b. Ask yourself: When my wife expresses hurt or anger, do I get defensive and angry, and then say, "Drop it. I don't want to talk about it"?

_____

_____

_____

_____

c. In his book *Love & Respect*, Emerson acknowledges that husbands find it tough to apologize. He explains: "As a husband I want to share with all husbands that I understand why it's hard to say, 'I'm sorry.' When a woman says, 'I'm sorry,' to her it's an increase of love. But when a man says, 'I'm sorry,' he fears that he will lose respect. This is especially true if he says he's sorry for something and then his wife brings it up again because she isn't convinced he means it. She simply thinks the issue is not resolved and it must be discussed some more; but he thinks she has just violated his honor code. . . . To all husbands I want to say, I've been there. I have had to push through and say to Sarah, 'I'm sorry. I was wrong.' And when I finally convinced her that I meant it, it healed her spirit. Those simple words put her at peace" (*Love & Respect*, Integrity, 2004, p. 161). Share your thoughts on Emerson's words.

_____

_____

_____

_____

d. Write a statement to your wife that will energize her when she is feeling a lack of peace in your relationship. (Page 192 has ideas you can adapt, or write your own.)

_____

_____

_____

_____

L – LOYALTY

7. Is she sure you'll always be there? A loving husband assures his wife of his love and commitment. He helps her feel secure in the covenant they have together. He

comforts her with the knowledge that he would never "deal treacherously" with her (see Malachi 2:14–15).

a. Agree or Disagree? Wives fear abandonment by their husbands. When your wife says, "Do you love me?" or "Will you love me forever?" she seeks reassurance of your loyalty.

_____

_____

_____

b. Ask yourself: Do I look for ways to express my loyalty to her, or do I think, *She knows I love her. I don't have to remind her?*

_____

_____

_____

c. In this "swimsuit issue" world, do I openly admire pretty women because I know my wife can handle it, or do I save my admiration for her? Do I understand that assurance of my loyalty calms her soul?

_____

_____

_____

d. List three ways to reassure your wife of your loyalty. Choose one and tell her ASAP If you need ideas, reread the section on Loyalty on pages 192–94.

_____

_____

_____

E – ESTEEM

8. A wife needs respect too. A loving husband honors and cherishes his wife in specific ways, making her feel she dwells first in his heart and honored as a "fellow heir of the grace of life" (1 Peter 3:7).

a. Ask yourself: Does my wife feel treasured by me?

_____

_____

_____

b. If your wife accusingly says, "You treat me like a doormat," do you decode her words as a cry for esteem and love? Or, do you feel she talks this way because she set her mind on belittling you?

_____

_____

_____

c. Do you take your wife's efforts with the family for granted, or do you express, "Thanks for everything you do for me and the kids. I could never, ever do your job!" Do you go beyond honoring her as an equal and point out the ways she betters you?

_____

_____

_____

d. Write an energizing remark that you will make to your wife today. (Refer to page 195 if you need ideas.)

_____

_____

_____

Teachability

9. All the decoding in the world won't help your marriage if you don't allow it to affect your behavior.

a. Back in Session One, you read C-O-U-P-L-E: A Checkup for Husbands. In question 6 of your assignment in Session One, you were asked to do an honest self-assessment on how you were showing love to your wife, based on the C-O-U-P-L-E principles. After digging into these principles more deeply this week, what grade would you give yourself?

_____

_____

b.   For the Risk Taker! Ask your wife what grade she gave you. Pray for an open
     heart to receive the insight she offers. Choose the area you need the most work
     on, and humbly ask the Lord to help you take practical steps this week to
     improve in that area. Write these steps in the space given, along with a day or
     time that you plan to apply them.

_____

_____

_____

_____

SESSION EIGHT

—◆—

In preparation for this session, please read Chapter Eleven, "Dealing with the Everyday Challenge" and Chapter Twelve, "More Strategies for Dealing with Communication Glitches."

We have just learned how important it is to decode our spouse's language. However, decoding is not the only skill you need to stay on the Energizing Cycle. Sometimes miscommunication happens when we fail to speak clearly or listen carefully. In this session, we will show how miscommunication might happen, and how to handle it when it does.

CHAPTER ELEVEN: "DEALING WITH THE EVERYDAY CHALLENGE"

The Back Patio

1. Read the story "All I Said Was 'I'm Leaving'" on pages 198–200.

   a. What does Emerson consider to be the "Everyday Challenge" that all married couples face?

   _____

   _____

   _____

   b. Outline how Emerson and Sarah experienced an "everyday challenge" to communicate, and how clarification came into play, if at all. Start by analyzing what each meant by the first words they spoke: Emerson—"I'm leaving." And Sarah—"Don't worry. I'm not coming out here to talk to you."

   _____

   _____

   _____

c. Think of a similar exchange that happened in the last day or two between you and your spouse. What took place?

_____

_____

_____

Rule #1

2. Not all misunderstandings are a Love and Respect issue.

a. Emerson's Rule No. 1 for Good Everyday Communication states: Take time to be clear. And to be clear, learn to speak carefully to be understood and, just as important, to listen carefully to understand (p. 200).

Agree or Disagree? If we would remember Rule No. 1, we could prevent most, if not all, daily communication from crossing the line and entering the Crazy Cycle.

_____

_____

b. Read the following scriptures (found on pages 198–206), and record the principle in each that supports Emerson's Rule No. 1.

1 Corinthians 14:9

_____

_____

2 Corinthians 11:6

_____

_____

Proverbs 18:13

_____

_____

Proverbs 15:28

_____

_____

Proverbs 16:23

_____

_____

Proverbs 25:15

_____

_____

James 1:19

_____

_____

Decoding Versus Clarifying

3. Decoding and clarifying differ.

   a. Explain the simple distinction between decoding and clarifying. Which
       description below describes decoding and which describes clarifying?

       1. _____ is what you do *before* you step on your mate's air hose
          and deflate his or her spirit. For example, when one of you isn't clear or isn't
          hearing correctly, then and there you _____ the misunderstanding
          before your spouse's spirit deflates (p. 202).

       2. _____ is what you do when you strongly suspect—or can
          clearly tell—that your mate's air hose has been pinched. You observe the spirit
          of your spouse deflate. You _____ that either she is feeling
          unloved or he is feeling disrespected. If you do not _____, the
          Crazy Cycle begins its spin!

   b. Going back to the story of Emerson and Sarah on the patio, did Emerson clarify
       Sarah's comment, "Don't worry. I'm not coming out here to talk to you"?

       _____

       _____

       _____

c. Had Sarah already misinterpreted Emerson's comment, "I'm leaving"? How might she have clarified his comment before responding?

_____

_____

_____

d. On pages 202–203, Emerson analyzes this patio conversation, explaining how their past marital dynamics contributed to the miscommunication. This illustrates that our past can influence us to mind-read and jump to conclusions about our spouse, leading us right onto the Crazy Cycle. As you reflect on the incident in question 1c, did either of you jump to conclusions based on the past? Did this trigger the Crazy Cycle? Why?

_____

_____

_____

Six Ideas on Feedback

4. Read "Using Feedback to Clarify Your Conversations" on page 346 in Appendix D in your *The Language of Love & Respect* book.

a. When giving feedback, which of the six following insights do you apply the most? The least?

1. *Always see your mate as an ally.* Feedback is of little use if you see your spouse as an enemy. Giving and receiving constructive feedback must assume goodwill in both partners. Both of you need to remember that, even if you don't always agree and even if you become irritated or angry, you are friends, and neither of you means to hurt the other.

2. *Whose problem is it, really?* When a husband or wife says, "We have communication problems!" what does that remark mean? Usually this means, "My spouse speaks or listens carelessly." People seldom think they cause the communication problem. They assume the best about themselves. But in our Love and Respect offices, we get letters from husbands and wives who earlier blamed their spouses for the communication problems but now take their share of the blame. In other words, your feedback improves when you take ownership for your role in the communication.

3. *Never assume you understand.* Giving and receiving feedback often involves emotions. When my conversations with Sarah start to get at all emotional, I have two rules:

Rule #1. I don't assume that I understand what Sarah said until she tells me that I did understand correctly.

Rule #2. I don't assume that Sarah understood what I said until she tells me what she heard me say and I verify it.

4. *You can skillfully make the first move.* If Sarah and I have even a glitch in communication, we both try to move first and take responsibility. We know we have goodwill. If we misunderstand, we assume that one of us probably didn't speak clearly enough or listen carefully enough. We stop the conversation, review the words, and straighten out the misunderstanding. We believe one of us has the skill to do something about our problems.

5. *Get the bee out of your glove.* How foolish to think you don't have the time or energy to give and receive feedback! In the best of marriages the bee of misunderstanding always buzzes about. To ignore misunderstanding is like a gardener who ignores a bee that flew into the cuff of her glove while she transplants some flowers. Before the bee stings, she needs to remove the glove! In marriage, expending time and energy on feedback removes the stings from misunderstanding.

6. *Use "I hear you saying" sparingly.* Feedback is not something new on the marital communication scene. It has been around for years, often called "active listening." Though responding with "I hear you saying . . ." followed by feedback is appropriate, be aware you can overdo this remark.

b. Which of the six ideas above does your spouse do the best? Be sure to thank them!

_____

_____

5. Marital researchers agree that a huge percentage of communication problems between husband and wife have less to do with *what* is said and more to do with *how* it is said—the attitude and tone of voice.

a. With men it is most often a stern and angry tone and expression, while with women it is most often contempt and condescension. Has your personal experience validated this observation? Explain your answer.

_____

_____

_____

_____

b. On page 207, Emerson found that a simple question asked by husband or wife before communication improves not only what is said but how it is said. Fill in the blanks below and commit the question to memory.

1. The husband should ask himself, "Is what I'm about to say going to result in my wife feeling _____ or _____?"

2. The wife should ask, "Is what I'm about to say going to result in my husband feeling _____ or _____?"

c. Will you prayerfully commit to put this question into action? For those keeping a journal, record the times you asked yourself this question and notice when your communication changed for the better.

_____

_____

CHAPTER TWELVE: "MORE STRATEGIES FOR DEALING WITH COMMUNICATION GLITCHES"

Careful Speaking, Careful Listening, and Mutual Understanding

6. After reading Chapter Twelve, did you put into practice the question: "Is what I'm about to say going to result in my spouse feeling loved or unloved / respected or disrespected?"

a. If you applied this question to your communication, explain what you noticed.

_____

_____

_____

_____

b. What two things does Emerson guarantee will happen if you use this question consistently?

_____

_____

_____

_____

c. Emerson writes, "When I listen more carefully, I tend to understand Sarah much better. In turn, she feels understood and is far less likely to be defensive. *She feels loved.* And when I speak more carefully, Sarah tends to understand me much better. When I feel understood, I am far less likely to be defensive. *I feel respected.*" Can you identify with Emerson's experience? Why?

_____

_____

_____

_____

Use Feedback to Clarify

7. Read the section entitled "When Glitches Come Up, Use Feedback to Clarify" (pp. 212–213).

a. Emerson writes, "Despite your best intentions, however, minor breakdowns or small glitches in communication do occur. When they happen, don't accuse your spouse of not listening carefully or speaking clearly." Why is this critical?

_____

_____

_____

_____

b. To provide feedback, do you do the following? Why or why not?

1. When your spouse seems unclear, you say, "I'm sorry. I guess I didn't understand. What I thought you said was . . . [Then state what you heard as best you can.] Is that correct?"

_____

_____

_____

_____

2. When you seem unclear to your spouse—your spouse either did not hear you correctly or has misinterpreted your words—you say, "I'm sorry. I was not as clear as I could have been. What I meant was . . . [Then restate what you are trying to convey as best you can.] Is that what you heard me saying?"

_____

_____

_____

_____

Women Remember Relational Words

8. Read "Why I Have Learned to 'Listen Up' More Often" (pp. 213–214).

a. Husbands, do you agree with Emerson's experience? "Based on my experience, I suggest to husbands that you refrain from arguing when your wife says, 'I did too say that.' Instead of claiming she didn't tell you clearly, admit that you probably didn't listen carefully enough. Trust her heart and give her the benefit of the doubt. If anything is to be doubted, it is probably your memory, because the typical male does not listen carefully to his wife. Fortunately, when I don't listen, Sarah cuts me some slack."

_____

_____

_____

b. Wives, do you give your husband slack? Why or why not?

_____

_____

_____

Talkative Wives

9. Read the sections entitled "Words of Caution for Talkative Wives . . ." and "A Word to the Wise for the Non-Talkative Husband" (pp. 214–220). Although husbands and wives should read both sections, resist the urge to use this information against your spouse.

a. **Wives:** Emerson cautions you not to interpret his teaching as license to demand that your husband talk every time you feel the need to talk. He encourages you to follow 1 Peter 3:1–6. Peter instructs wives to show a quiet spirit and to win a husband without a word. As you consider Peter's words, what questions come to your mind? Write them here for discussion with your husband and/or group.

    _____

    _____

    _____

b. In your opinion, why does God expect you to obey the truths in 1 Peter 3:1–6? What benefits you when applying these truths?

    _____

    _____

    _____

c. Emerson says that many women conclude, because of the conditioning of feminism, that silence causes them to lose power and their sense of self. Yet, God instructs with divine wisdom and purpose in 1 Peter 3:1–6. What fears surface for you when you read this passage? What can you do with these fears?

    _____

    _____

    _____

d. How does Emerson's feedback from husbands across the country reinforce that 1 Peter 3:1–6 is God's wisdom for wives (p. 217)? Men, explain why less talking from wives might communicate more.

    _____

    _____

    _____

Non-Talkative Husbands

10. From pages 217–20, read "A Word to the Wise for the Non-Talkative Husband." Although husbands and wives should read both sections, resist the urge to use this information against your spouse.

   a. **Husbands:** Emerson cautions you to not interpret his suggestion that your wife talks a lot as confirmation that you get off the hook. Although Peter instructs wives to do less talking, he directs husbands to live with their wives in an understanding way (1 Peter 3:7). Though you talk less, should you listen less?

   Note: To grasp the meaning of the phrase "as with a weaker vessel" (1 Peter 3:7), read the footnote on page 324 (Chapter 12, number 2). What do you think Peter meant by "weaker vessel"?

   _____

   _____

   _____

   _____

   b. Do you agree or disagree that Peter instructs a husband to understand his wife because by nature the typical male overlooks his wife's need for understanding and fails to see how this causes his wife to feel loved? Explain your answer.

   _____

   _____

   _____

   _____

   c. Peter continues in 1 Peter 3:7 by commanding husbands to grant their wives "honor as a fellow heir of the grace of life, so that your prayers will not be hindered." Have you recognized that when you dishonor your wife, this hinders your prayers? For example, will God listen to you talk to Him if you consistently chastise your wife by bellowing, "I don't have to put up with all your useless yakking!"?

   _____

   _____

   _____

   _____

d. After reading Emerson's man-to-man thoughts on what he learned about how to live with a wife in an understanding way (pp. 218–219), what hit home for you? Did you see yourself in the examples of what not to do? Write down one area that needs your immediate attention and application.

_____

_____

_____

_____

e. **Husbands and Wives:** As an honorable man seeking to honor his wife and as a loving wife seeking to respect her husband, how might you shape your marriage with not too much talking but not too little talking? Write down your suggestions here for discussion with your spouse and/or group.

_____

_____

_____

_____

Spiderwebbing

11. We can all identify with and find humor in the truth about a wife's "spiderwebbing." Read pages 220–22.

a. Husbands, what did you learn about spiderwebbing that helps you understand your wife?

_____

_____

_____

_____

b. Wives, what did you learn about spiderwebbing that helps you understand your husband?

_____

_____

_____

_____

You Will Have Trouble

12. Read 1 Corinthians 7:28 (p. 223).

    a. What important truth does this scripture make known?

       _____

       _____

       _____

       _____

    b. Although this verse sounds discouraging to some, many couples find encouragement. Because their marriage has troubles does not mean their marriage is "bad." A common theme throughout God's Word is that strength of character comes from trouble and conflict. A marriage matures through conflict. Though a marital problem troubles you, is God using this for your good and maturity as you trust and obey Him? Write out your thoughts.

       _____

       _____

       _____

       _____

    c. Take some time to go back over this session and take note of the applications to which you have committed. As a couple, share with each other (lovingly and respectfully!) what you learned about yourself.

    d. Optional: If ready, take the next step and risk listening to what your spouse thinks you can do to better your everyday communication.

PART FIVE: THE REWARDED CYCLE: THE UNCONDITIONAL DIMENSION OF COMMUNICATION

SESSION NINE

In this session, we start Part V, The Rewarded Cycle: The Unconditional Dimension of Communication. In Part III, we learned how to slow or stop the Crazy Cycle by learning each other's language, leading to mutual understanding and, in the end, better communication. In Part IV, we learned how to get on the Energizing Cycle by putting the principles in C-O-U-P-L-E and C-H-A-I-R-S into practice.

However, beyond mutual understanding and good communication, marriage has an unseen facet. This dimension is what this book is about—that marriage is less about our relationship to our spouse and more about our relationship to God. And when we learn to communicate in marriage God's way, with words of unconditional love and respect, God rewards us even when our spouse does not respond! This is the essence of the Rewarded Cycle:

HIS LOVING WORDS BLESS REGARDLESS OF HER RESPECTFUL WORDS.

HER RESPECTFUL WORDS BLESS REGARDLESS OF HIS LOVING WORDS.

CHAPTER THIRTEEN: "WHY THE REWARDED CYCLE IS FOR EVERY MARRIAGE—HOT, COLD, OR LUKEWARM"

In the next four chapters, we will enter the unconditional dimension of life called God's kingdom. In this sphere, couples speak unconditional words of love and respect for

Christ and to Christ. Let's start by reading Chapter Thirteen, "Why the Rewarded Cycle Is for Every Marriage—Hot, Cold, or Lukewarm."

Communication Is Not about Your Spouse

1. Marital communication goes beyond your marriage! As a follower of Christ, marital communication requires that you talk the way God calls you to talk, even to an unresponsive spouse.

   a. In the introduction to Part V Emerson writes, "I made the point that the key to marriage is not communication per se. The real key is mutual understanding, which is gained by learning to speak each other's language, with the husband speaking love to his wife and the wife speaking respect to her husband. And as they better understand each other, better communication has to follow. While all of that is certainly true, there is a dimension to marriage that goes beyond mutual understanding and good communication. In an ultimate sense, this book is not primarily about either one, because your marriage is not only about your relationship to your spouse. First and foremost, your marriage is about your relationship to God and communicating the way He commands" (pp. 225–226).

      Do you agree or disagree with this idea? Why?

      _____

      _____

      _____

      _____

   b. "God's way of communicating in marriage is to talk with words of unconditional love and respect. When you speak words of love and respect, God rewards you. In fact, He rewards you even if your spouse does not respond positively to your words of love and respect. This is what the Rewarded Cycle is all about" (p. 226).

      Do you believe this? Why or why not?

      _____

      _____

      _____

   c. "Unconditional words of love or respect do not mean you turn a blind eye to your spouse's wrongdoing. However, you speak the truth lovingly or respectfully. This is the gift you give your spouse. Your spouse has not earned this gracious confrontation, and it certainly isn't in your nature to give such a gift! Your propensity, if you are like the rest of us, is to give your spouse a well-deserved tongue lashing—a lashing that is biting and insulting. But you pull back from this manner of scolding because of the Lord's commandment to you not to talk this way. God has revealed a different way to communicate, and He rewards this way of talking" (pp. 226–227).

What are your thoughts on the above? Have you learned to apply unconditional speech, and if so, how?

_____

_____

_____

_____

Talking to God

2. As a follower of Christ, to talk to your spouse with love or respect you need to talk to God first, depending on Him in prayer!

a. Communication with God exceeds in importance your communication with your spouse. After all, your spouse might turn a deaf ear toward you and refuse to communicate. That is why you must realize the need for prayer—talking to God, sharing your burdens, and getting His support and strength to love or respect. In your marriage, have you experienced such communication with God? If you depended on God, what were the results?

_____

_____

_____

_____

b. Write a sentence or two that describes your communication with God.

_____

_____

_____

c. Write a sentence or two that describes your communication with your spouse.

_____

_____

_____

_____

d. Do you notice a connection? Does one influence the other? Explain.

_____

_____

_____

_____

When There Is No Reciprocity!

3. Your spouse will not always respond as you expect.

a. Emerson writes, "We know from personal experience that no couple can keep the Energizing Cycle going without a hitch. Just because Sarah speaks respectful words does not guarantee I will be motivated to respond with a love song. . . . Sarah could easily say, 'Well, I've done my part. Now it's his turn to make the first move and get us back on track.' But suppose I'm stubborn and don't make any kind of move, such as saying, 'I'm sorry'? Maybe I am so wrapped up in my own thinking I'm not even aware of what I have said that is so unloving. Or I could have made a very loving remark to Sarah and, for any number of reasons, gotten disrespect in return. This kind of less-than-perfect talking and acting happens in the best of marriages."

Give an example of your "less-than-perfect talking."

_____

_____

_____

_____

b. Give an example of when you spoke words of love/respect although your spouse did not respond. Did you stop talking with love/respect or stick with it? Explain what happened.

_____

_____

_____

_____

Unto Christ

4. All Christ followers must talk as "unto Christ."

a. When talking to your spouse, do you picture talking to Christ? Do you see Him, with the eyes of faith, standing beyond the shoulder of your spouse? Choose one of these three answers:

   1. Yes
   2. No
   3. Sometimes

b. How would things change in your marriage if you treated your spouse as you would treat Christ? What would happen if you talked with love and respect because Christ was listening?

_____

_____

_____

_____

Ted and Tammy

5. The Rewarded Cycle is the essence of the Love and Respect message! Yet grasping and applying this revolutionary message can be difficult. Read the story of Ted and Tammy starting on page 233.

a. What did it take for the truth in the Rewarded Cycle to sink in for Ted?

_____

_____

_____

_____

b. What happened when Ted realized he would never treat his customers as he treated his wife and children?

_____

_____

_____

_____

Ephesians 6:8

6. Paul had your marriage in mind when he wrote Ephesians 6:7–8: "Serve wholeheartedly, as if you were serving the Lord, not men, because you know that the Lord will reward everyone for whatever good he does, whether he is slave or free" (NIV). If you trace his thinking to the previous verses, you find him mentioning children and their parents (Ephesians 6:1–4) and husbands and wives (Ephesians 5:22–33). Paul is saying that whatever you do for the Lord you get back from the Lord.

a. In marriage, how do you get back from the Lord when you love or respect unto Him, even when your spouse ignores your love or respect?

_____

_____

_____

_____

b. Explain how this illustrates the Rewarded Cycle.

_____

_____

_____

_____

Who Is Rewarded?

7. Whether you enjoy a good marriage or suffer in a struggling marriage, the Rewarded Cycle—the unconditional dimension—applies to every believer in Christ.

   a. Agree or Disagree? A couple could grow up in a secular home, conditioned to speak with anger and sarcasm, yet later choose to speak with words of love and respect because of their love and reverence for Christ. On the other hand, a couple could grow up in a Christian home, conditioned to speak with love and respect, yet this couple rarely speaks from a love and reverence for Christ.

   b. This first couple (in "7a") rates 6 on a 10-point scale for speaking with love and respect in marriage. They carry on as a work in progress! The second couple rates 7 on a 10-point scale for speaking words of love and respect. Their cultural Christianity equipped them to speak with love and respect. Yet the first couple obtains God's reward because they started at 2 and by faith in Christ progressed to 6, whereas the second couple started at 8 because of their parents' influence but regressed to 7 because faith in Jesus did not drive their marital communication.

      Why should this illustration encourage the first couple and convict the second?

      _____

      _____

      _____

      _____

      What does this uncover about the danger of comparing your marriage to the marriage of others (2 Corinthians 10:12)?

      _____

      _____

      _____

      _____

   c. The Rewarded Cycle reminds us that our conscious desire to obey Christ becomes the motive for speaking with words of love and respect. To what extent do you understand and apply this?

      Very much   So-so   Very little

Scriptures about the Unconditional

8. No matter the condition of your marriage, when you grasp the meaning of the Rewarded Cycle and apply the truth, you move into the "Unconditional Dimension."

   a.   Look up the following scriptures, and record how these Bible verses support the truth that God rewards you for living in the unconditional dimension.

   Matthew 5:11–12

   _____
   _____
   _____

   Matthew 5:46–47

   _____
   _____
   _____

   Hebrews 10:35

   _____
   _____
   _____

   1 Peter 2:18–23

   _____
   _____
   _____

   1 Peter 3:9

   _____
   _____
   _____

   1 Peter 4:14

   _____
   _____
   _____

b. Of these scriptures, which have you applied to your marriage? Which verse inspires you the most?

_____

_____

_____

Testimonies of the Unconditional

9. To respond with unconditional love or respect when your spouse is mistreating you sounds impossible. But God's Word teaches that you can live in the unconditional realm! Christ Himself set the example for you. Remember, God never sets you up for failure, taking delight in your stumbling as though He is some kind of cosmic killjoy. He promises to help you! He promises to never leave you or forsake you. Hope and trust in God is what will keep you on the Rewarded Cycle when it is the last thing you feel you can do.

a. Read the real-life stories of couples who experienced the unconditional dimension. Look at pages 237–44. What do the husbands and wives in these stories share?

_____

_____

_____

_____

b. Because of your partner's free will, there are no guarantees that your marriage will turn around, even if you practice the Rewarded Cycle. How did the husbands and wives in these stories face the reality of no guarantees?

_____

_____

_____

_____

Well Done!

10. When you love or respect your spouse unconditionally, as unto Christ, rewards come to you. But not all rewards come to you on earth. Read the section entitled "Rewards Here Pale in Comparison to Rewards There" on page 244 to the end of the chapter.

a. Take a moment to reflect on the end of your life as you stand before God. Imagine hearing the words, "Well done, good and faithful servant!" What comes to your mind when you think of hearing these words?

_____

_____

_____

_____

b. Though you see little results of your unconditional love and respect on earth, do you get a glimpse of the reward coming to you in heaven? Explain.

_____

_____

_____

_____

Happy or Holy?

Emerson warns against following the voices of worldly wisdom that support "being happy" over "being holy." The following scriptures encourage faithfulness and holiness. Choose the ones that speak to you, and write them on an index card or Post-it note as a reminder to never, ever give up! (You may wish to look at these verses on pages 243–47).

2 Chronicles 15:7

Matthew 12:36–37

Matthew 25:21

2 Corinthians 4:17–18

Galatians 6:9

Colossians 3:23–24

2 John 8

Revelation 22:12

SESSION TEN

CHAPTER FOURTEEN: "THE JESUS WAY OF TALKING—PART I: COMMUNICATING WITH LOVE AND RESPECT"

In preparation for this session, read Chapter Fourteen, "The Jesus Way of Talking—Part I: Communicating with Love and Respect."

In Session Nine, we talked about the Rewarded Cycle and living in the unconditional dimension. But how can we apply the Rewarded Cycle to the mouth? In this session, we will discover the Jesus Way of Talking—five types of speech that please God. As we learn to speak the Jesus Way in marriage, God rewards us—here, and in Eternity!

The Triangle

1. In Session Two you paid special attention to the idea that what comes out of your mouth matters. Your words publicize the state of your heart (Luke 6:45). Furthermore, the Lord of heaven and earth listens!

   Emerson shares the following story of how he saw this realization come to his father: *I was eighteen when my father placed his faith in Jesus Christ. He was fifty-one, and the first change I noticed in him was his vocabulary. He simply stopped cursing and using profanity. . . . Dad quickly recognized the hypocrisy in saying he was a believer and going into profane rages. My father understood that if he wanted to obey and please God, he could not continue to give free rein to his anger and talk as he had before. Now that he was saved, Dad had two relationships—one with Mom and one with God—and he realized that neither was separate from the other. He could not talk to God one way and to my mother another. To my knowledge, Dad never went into another rage like the ones that were commonplace for him before he became a follower of Christ (pp. 249–250).*

a. Why did Emerson's dad change? Do you relate to his dad? Have you thought about the triangle of you, your spouse, and God?

   _____

   _____

   _____

   _____

b. James writes about the tongue: "With it we bless our Lord and Father, and with it we curse people who are made in the likeness of God. From the same mouth come blessing and cursing. My brothers, these things ought not to be so" (James 3:9–10 ESV). If you praise God on Sunday and spew words of hate and contempt at your spouse on Monday, which words tell the condition of your heart?

   _____

   _____

   _____

   _____

c. James says, "If anyone thinks himself to be religious, and yet does not bridle his tongue but deceives his *own* heart, this man's religion is worthless" (James 1:26). How is he fooling himself, and why is his religion worthless?

   _____

   _____

   _____

   _____

Make Me a Blessing!

2. God rewards you for speaking positive and unconditional words. (Read "What If My Spouse Doesn't Deserve My Blessing?" on page 252.)

   a. Think of the words you recently spoke to your spouse on the heels of your mate stepping on your air hose. Did you speak words of blessing?

   _____

   _____

   _____

   _____

b. According to 1 Peter 3:9, what should motivate you to give a blessing? "Not returning evil for evil or insult for insult, but giving a blessing instead; for you were called for the very purpose that you might inherit a blessing" (1 Peter 3:9).

_____

_____

_____

_____

c. In 1 Corinthians 4:12 we read, "When we are reviled, we bless." How do you bless a spouse who reviles and insults you?

_____

_____

_____

_____

d. One definition of a blessing is giving people something that helps them feel thankful, secure, supported, content, or encouraged. What if you knew your spouse struggled with insecurities about your love and respect? At a weak moment, your spouse wrongly accused you of failing to love or respect him/her. You felt reviled and insulted. What would happen if you replied, "I'm sorry. Will you forgive me?" Why would this qualify as a blessing?

_____

_____

_____

_____

Talk "As to the Lord"

3. Last session we asked you, "When talking to your spouse, do you picture talking to Christ? Do you see Him, with the eyes of faith, standing beyond the shoulder of your spouse?" We asked you to evaluate yourself. Let's reconsider this foundational truth.

a. Think of a typical moment when you get frustrated with your spouse. Envision Jesus standing beyond the shoulder of your spouse. During the moment of frustration, see yourself speaking not only to your spouse but to Jesus. Does this image of Jesus listening to you help you talk differently?

_____

_____

_____

_____

b. What do the following scriptures say to you?

Matthew 25:40: "Verily I say unto you, inasmuch as ye have done it unto one of the least of these my brethren, ye have done it unto me" (KJV).

_____

_____

_____

_____

Ephesians 5:22: "Wives . . . as to the Lord."

_____

_____

_____

_____

Ephesians 6:5: "as to Christ"

_____

_____

_____

_____

Ephesians 6:7: "as to the Lord, and not to men . . ."

_____

_____

_____

_____

c. In Colossians 3:17 Paul writes, "Whatever you do, in word or deed, do everything in the name of the Lord Jesus"(ESV). And in Colossians 3:23–24 he pens, "Whatever you do, work heartily, as for the Lord and not for men, knowing that from the Lord you will receive the inheritance as your reward. You are serving the Lord Christ" (ESV). Put into your own words what Paul is asking you to do in these verses.

_____

_____

_____

_____

d. Make this commitment: "With God's help, the next time I get frustrated with my spouse, I will speak words of love or respect 'as to the Lord' for His reward! And when I fail, I will apologize since I am also confessing to Jesus who stands beyond the shoulder of my spouse."

Talk as the Lord Talked

4. Emerson discovered the Ephesians learned from Christ five ways of talking.

When writing about marriage in Ephesians 5:22–33, Paul does not deal with the mouth. This baffled Emerson until he looked in the verses just before. In Ephesians 4:20–5:21, Paul addresses the use of the lips five times. In each instance, he teaches the Ephesians, and therefore us, to stop talking in a bad way and start talking in a good way. He refers to this as putting off the "old self" and putting on the "new self." In fact, the "new self" speaks according to "the likeness of God" (Ephesians 4:24), whereas the "old self" speaks in ways that do not reflect God's likeness. About the "old self" Paul points out that the Ephesians "did not learn Christ in this way" (Ephesians 4:20). In other words, the old self does not show the Jesus way of talking.

a. What is the God-like or Jesus Way of Talking? Read Ephesians 4:20–5:21, then spell out the following acronym with each word and corresponding verse.

T_____ – (Ephesians 4:25)

U _____ – (Ephesians 4:29)

F _____ – (Ephesians 4:31–32)

T _____ – (Ephesians 5:4)

S _____ – (Ephesians 5:19)

b. What must guide words of love and respect? Fill in the blanks below with T-U-F-T-S.

Words of love or respect must include _____ because your spouse is bound to fail you.

Words of love or respect must _____ your spouse, edifying—and never manipulating—him or her.

Words of love or respect must be _____ because lies and half truths will undermine your relationship.

Words of love or respect must be based and focused on _____; avoid ideas that are contrary to the heart of Christ.

Words of love or respect must include _____ spoken to or about your spouse; refusing to fixate on weaknesses and faults.

c. Did you know you can talk like Jesus talked (T-U-F-T-S) yet your spouse may not respond positively? (Remember, not everyone responded positively to the words of Jesus, and Jesus talked like Jesus!) Share your thoughts on this.

_____

_____

_____

_____

If you feel discouraged at your inability to talk as Jesus talked, take heart! God always equips us for the tasks that lie before us. Ask God, in a moment of silence, to help you talk the way Jesus talked.

This Isn't about Your Spouse

5. Emerson closes Chapter Fourteen with these sobering words: "Your spouse may chide you, criticize you, or even abuse you verbally, but your spouse cannot make you sin with your lips. That is your decision. Your reactions to your spouse will reveal to God your commitment to speak in a way that blesses Him and results in an eternal reward for you. The way to bless God and your mate with your words is to practice T-U-F-T-S, which is really foundational to practicing Love and Respect" (p. 264). The commitment to talk the Jesus Way makes you a Love and Respect communicator.

a. Prayerfully consider which of the following the Lord would have you apply.

  1. Truthful words
  2. Uplifting words
  3. Forgiving words
  4. Thankful words
  5. Scriptural words

b. What is hindering you from applying T-U-F-T-S in obedience to the Lord?

  _____

  _____

  _____

  _____

  Confess to God the barrier to your commitment to T-U-F-T-S. Remember, your spouse is not causing you to disobey God.

A Tiny Drop of Poison

6. Many e-mails come to Emerson each month from individuals trying to speak lovingly or respectfully. However, at times they fail to see that their speech goes against T-U-F-T-S. For example, Monday through Friday a person can speak with love and respect, but on Saturday this person's lie poisons the marriage. A little leaven leavens the whole (1 Corinthians 5:6); that is, a tiny drop of poison in a large glass of milk still kills.

  a. Which one of the following have you seen in another couple? Don't name names!

  1. Truthful (Ephesians 4:25):
     Though George thinks of himself as a husband who speaks lovingly, he hedges on the truth. He spends money they don't have but tells Ruthie, his wife, the checkbook balances just fine.

  2. Uplifting (Ephesians 4:29):
     Kelly speaks respectfully to her husband, Eric, but her motive is to change him. Trying to get Eric to love her in romantic ways, she uses respect talk as another new formula, not as a means designed by God to meet a need in Eric.

3. Forgiving (Ephesians 4:31–32):
   Heather speaks respectfully to Josh but mentally fixates on a dozen things about him she resents, like his leaving dirty dishes in the sink. She voices to her mom that Josh causes her unhappiness and she deserves someone better.

4. Thankful (Ephesians 5:4):
   In the home Will tries to speak in loving ways to his wife, Tonya, but with friends Tonya becomes the butt of his jokes. She tells him that she feels devalued and unappreciated. He laughs off her complaint.

5. Scriptural (Ephesians 5:19):
   A husband and wife try to speak lovingly or respectfully but the thought surfaces, "I don't feel like speaking these words. My spouse irks me and is undeserving."

b. When reading this list of five ways of talking, did you think of your own marriage? If so, what did you think?

_____

_____

_____

c. Did you read the above examples of T-U-F-T-S judging your spouse or judging yourself? Why? If both, to whom did you give the most mercy?

_____

_____

_____

Dispositional Versus Situational

7. Emerson writes, "Why do husbands and wives tend to favor themselves when someone's air hose gets pinched? One psychological explanation is rooted in the dispositional versus the situational perspective on conversations. If your spouse speaks in a hurtful way, it is natural to conclude that the hurtful words were caused by your spouse's lousy disposition; your spouse (more's the pity) has some real character flaws. But, of course, when you say something that is hurtful, it is natural for you to conclude it was not your fault; it was simply caused by the situation at hand. You were a victim of circumstances" (p. 260).

a.   In your own words, explain the dispositional-versus-situational thinking.

_____

_____

_____

_____

b.   Ask yourself the questions Emerson asks: "Do I let myself off the hook for my reactions and comments, which are just as negative and damaging as anything my spouse might do or say? Do I give myself grace and my spouse judgment?" (p. 263).

_____

_____

_____

_____

c.   Read Matthew 7:1–5. With the above questions in mind, how do these verses speak to you?

_____

_____

_____

_____

The Checklist

8. God has given us a guide or checklist for talking.

a.   Tell why this is true: T-U-F-T-S serves as a checklist in preventing you from overlooking the ways you undermine love and respect in your marriage. Also, the Jesus Way of Talking helps you battle tendencies to second-guess yourself because it gives you guidelines for your words.

_____

_____

_____

_____

b. Give your thoughts on the following statement: In God's eyes you can communicate with words of love and respect even when your spouse doesn't listen.

_____

_____

_____

_____

Say Something ASAP!

9. You can apply some aspect of T-U-F-T-S immediately "as to the Lord"!

a. **Husbands,** which of the following will you say as soon as possible "as to the Lord"? Make a mental note of one and then follow through.

1. Speak Truthfully about a weakness of yours in applying something from C-O-U-P-L-E
2. Speak Upliftingly about a need of your wife's in C-O-U-P-L-E. Validating this need edifies her.
3. Speak Forgivingly about your wife's struggle to apply C-H-A-I-R-S.
4. Speak Thankfully about something your wife applied from C-H-A-I-R-S.
5. Speak Scripturally about her need for love. Let her know that God's Word teaches you that she needs love.

b. **Wives,** which of the following will you say as soon as possible "as to the Lord"? Make a mental note of which one and then follow through.

1. Speak Truthfully about a weakness of yours in applying something from C-H-A-I-R-S.
2. Speak Upliftingly about a need of your husband's in C-H-A-I-R-S. Validating this need edifies him.
3. Speak Forgivingly about your husband's struggle to apply C-O-U-P-L-E.
4. Speak Thankfully about something your husband applied from C-O-U-P-L-E.
5. Speak Scripturally about his need for respect. Let him know that God's Word teaches you that he needs respect.

SESSION ELEVEN

CHAPTER FIFTEEN: "THE JESUS WAY OF TALKING—PART II: TO LOVE AND RESPECT, USE TRUTHFUL, UPLIFTING, AND FORGIVING WORDS"

In preparation for this session, read Chapter Fifteen, "The Jesus Way of Talking—Part II: To Love and Respect: Use Truthful, Uplifting, and Forgiving Words."

The Car Salesman

1. Emerson writes, "Lying or evil words come from the heart. For example, what do you get when a lying, alcoholic used-car salesman stops drinking? A lying, sober used-car salesman. This is not to say a liar cannot stop lying, but it does mean that such a person must confess that lying is deep in the DNA of his or her being. Lying is not caused by one's surroundings.

   "Note that truthful or good words also come from the heart. Listen in as a man courts a widow. Her first husband was a habitual liar, and naturally she is prompted to ask, 'If I marry you, will you always speak truthfully to me?' He replies, 'Whether you marry me or not, I will speak truthfully.' It would do this widow well to give this man strong consideration as a possible husband. He is telling her that he will always speak truthfully because he has chosen to be a truthful person. Good fruit comes from a good root."

   a. Do you agree or disagree with what Emerson writes above? Why?

   _____

   _____

   _____

   _____

   b. In Matthew 12:33–35 (NIV), Jesus says: "Make a tree good and its fruit will be good, or make a tree bad and its fruit will be bad, for a tree is recognized by its fruit. You brood of vipers, how can you who are evil say anything good? For out of the overflow of the heart the mouth speaks. The good man brings good things out of the good stored up in him, and the evil man brings evil things out of the evil stored up in him." How does this apply to the car salesman and the man courting the widow?

_____

_____

_____

_____

T – TRUTHFUL WORDS: Always speak the truth, since the smallest of lies discredits your words of love or respect.

2. Truthful Words make up the first step in the Jesus Way of Talking.

   a. Agree or Disagree, and why? Once a person is caught in a lie, no matter how big or how small, trust is damaged.

   _____

   _____

   _____

   _____

   b. Jesus and His disciples addressed truthfulness. Look up the following verses and paraphrase the main point in each:

   John 8:44

   _____

   _____

   _____

   _____

   Matthew 12:33–35

   _____

   _____

   _____

   _____

Acts 5:4

_____

_____

_____

_____

Ephesians 4:25

_____

_____

_____

_____

c. Write a sentence or two about how these scriptures apply to your marriage.

_____

_____

_____

_____

Honest to God

3. Lying or evil words come from the heart, just as truthful or good words come from the heart. Yet even believers in a Christian marriage can get caught in a web of deceit.

   a. Enter a moment of quiet self-examination. Have you lied to your spouse? Ask yourself why.

   _____

   _____

   _____

   b. Because you hurt the heart of God by your lies, what untruthfulness do you need to confess to the Lord? Will God forgive you (1 John 1:9)?

   _____

   _____

   _____

c. Agree or Disagree? Though God forgives you in Christ and loves you unconditionally, He will not allow you to lie without consequences. God's love compels Him, like a good parent, to discipline (not punish) you for those lies that hurt you, your marriage, and Him.

Confessing to Your Spouse

4. Deception is a weighty matter. Coming clean is vital.

a. Agree or Disagree? When you confess the truth after exposure, this strikes your spouse as insincere.

b. What dishonesty do you need to confess to your spouse to start the Jesus Way of Talking (James 5:16)?
    Note: We are not talking about confessing a little white lie like, "I should have told you that you looked fat in that red dress but instead I said you looked great. I confess. I lied. You looked fat." This is serious. For example, "I need to confess an untruth I told you. I blamed you for my unloving reaction by claiming you disrespected me. I misled you. I blamed you to justify my unloving actions. Will you forgive me?"

    _____

    _____

    _____

    _____

c. Before confessing a serious sin, like adultery, the guilty party should get outside guidance from a godly, competent counselor to approach the innocent spouse with wisdom. For example, though you need to confess in order to obey Christ and clear your conscience, think about the pain your confession will inflict upon your spouse. Things could go from bad to worse. You might be ill-prepared for the backlash. With good counsel, you can approach with wisdom. Ask yourself, "To whom should I turn for counsel?"

d. Some of you feel unhappy about your marriage, yet there is nothing seriously wrong between you and your spouse. For instance, there is no lying. You have a truthful and good marriage. You can fail to see how horrific things could be. Rejoice and express your gratefulness to God and your spouse!

Your Insecurity

5. Some of you married an honest person. At the beginning of the marriage, your spouse spoke the truth. After a couple of years, you noticed your mate withholding information. Why? When speaking the truth to you in love and respect, you shut down. You did not want to hear the truth about yourself or your spouse. Threatened by the information, you silenced your spouse through your insecurity and anger. Today, your spouse tiptoes around you while you profile your spouse as dishonest.

   a. Do you identify with this assessment?

   _____

   _____

   b. Do you need to acknowledge that the issue is not that your spouse lies but that you sent a message that you did not want to hear the truth?

   _____

   _____

The Commitment

6. If you wish to stop hedging on the truth, you need to commit to truthfulness.

   The Commitment:

   Lies are incompatible with the Jesus Way of Talking. Lying is not the way I learned Christ. Jesus always speaks what is true, and so will I.

U – UPLIFTING WORDS: Always speak in an uplifting way for your spouse's sake and do not use love or respect as a manipulative ploy to meet your own need for love or respect.

7. The second letter in our acronym T-U-F-T-S stands for Uplifting Words.

   a. Read the following scriptures and summarize the main point in each:

   Ephesians 4:29

   _____

   _____

   _____

1 Thessalonians 5:11

_____

_____

_____

Psalm 141:3

_____

_____

_____

Proverbs 16:2

_____

_____

_____

b. Write a sentence or two on how these scriptures speak to you, especially about your marriage.

_____

_____

_____

How One Husband Spoke Uplifting Words

8. Read the example of "How One Husband Builds Up His Wife" on pages 271–73. Although written from a husband's perspective, the ideas apply also to a wife.

   a. While Gary's illustrations might seem "over the top," try not to get overwhelmed. Instead, ask yourself what ideas you can glean from this example to apply in your own marriage. Write two or three specific ways you can uplift your spouse this week.

   _____

   _____

   _____

   b. The opposite of uplifting words is critical words. If your spouse criticizes and tears you down, choosing to uplift in return is challenging! Have you been on the receiving end of harsh criticism from your spouse? How does the Rewarded Cycle help you in this situation?

_____

_____

_____

_____

c. When you think about speaking unconditional words that uplift your spouse, what are your questions and struggles?

_____

_____

_____

_____

d. Perhaps you are the one dishing out criticism. Take a moment to think about how you speak to your spouse. Would you speak this way to a friend? Have you thought about what your critical words are doing to your spouse's spirit? Even if your spouse "deserves it," what might happen if you chose to give your spouse a blessing rather than criticism? What would that look like?

_____

_____

_____

_____

The Wife Who Mothers Her Husband

9. In the section on "Why Wives Tend to Mother Their Husbands" (pp. 275–277), Emerson challenges women to evaluate their expectations for a perfect marriage.

a. Wives, is this perfectionist tendency something to which you can relate? If so, jot down specifically how you have struggled with this.

_____

_____

_____

_____

b.   How will you remedy this? (Read page 277 for ideas.)

_____

_____

_____

_____

c.   Husbands, when speaking the truth to your wife, do you also speak uplifting words? If you are not uplifting, what do you need to do to remedy this? (See Emerson's reference to "Don't beat the sheep" on page 277.)

_____

_____

_____

_____

Manipulation

10. Occasionally, Emerson hears from a person whose spouse uses the Love and Respect message to manipulate.

a.   Have you used uplifting words to get your way?

_____

_____

_____

b.   How might this manipulation affect your marriage? What do you feel when manipulated by "uplifting" words?

_____

_____

_____

Stiff-Arming

11. Your spouse could genuinely seek to build you up but your melancholy state downplays the affirming words.

a. Has your spouse tried to lift you up but you stopped your spouse from encouraging you? Have you countered your spouse's positive words with, "That's not true!" Why?

_____

_____

_____

_____

b. Should you seek your spouse's forgiveness for stiff-arming their attempts to edify you? If yes, when will you apologize?

_____

_____

_____

_____

The Commitment

12. Wholesome speech edifies and builds up. Couples who succeed with good verbal communication affirm the positive. Is God calling you to commit to uplifting words?

The Commitment:

Tearing down my spouse is not the Jesus Way of Talking. Building up my spouse is the way I learned Christ. Jesus gave grace to those who heard Him, using Uplifting Words to meet their needs, and so will I.

F – FORGIVING WORDS: Knowing my spouse will not be able to love or respect me perfectly, I commit to having a forgiving spirit so that I may never speak hatefully or contemptuously.

13. Back in Session Five, you were challenged to look deep into your heart to see if you were harboring unforgiveness. If you have resentments, please open your heart to the power of forgiveness. Consider the F in T-U-F-T-S: Forgiving Words.

a. How do you react when your spouse is unloving or disrespectful?

_____

_____

_____

_____

b. How often do you act on this statement? "Knowing my spouse will not love or respect me perfectly, I show a forgiving spirit so that I won't speak hatefully or contemptuously."

All the time   Sometimes   Rarely

Resentment

14. True forgiveness can't coexist with resentment.

a. Think back over the past weeks since you did Session Five on forgiveness. Have you put away "all bitterness and wrath and anger and clamor and slander . . . along with all malice" (Ephesians 4:31)? If so, how have you stayed free of bitterness?

_____

_____

_____

_____

b. Do you follow 1 Peter 3:9, not returning evil for evil, but giving a blessing instead? Assess yourself. If you are failing, ask the Lord to help you. Remember, He loves you and has forgiven you.

_____

_____

_____

_____

Overly Sensitive

15. Situations arise in marriage where you could resent your spouse without justification. Your hurt feelings do not prove your spouse has in fact offended you.

a. Read the following statements, and note whether you agree or disagree. If you see yourself in these statements, write your thoughts about what you need to do to change.

1. Emerson points out that if you continuously feel offended in the gray areas, you possess a judgmental spirit. When resentment overcomes you on an issue that is not moral, dangerous, or abusive, this is your issue.

   _____

2. If you struggle to forgive your spouse for normal marital tensions, this is far less about your spouse and more about you expecting paradise on earth. You expect your spouse to meet all your needs.

   _____

b. If your spouse unfairly criticizes you, why is it unwise to say, "You are overly sensitive and judgmental"?

_____

_____

_____

The Challenge

16. Emerson ends this important section on using forgiving words with a sobering challenge: "How Unforgiveness Can Lead to Slander" (pp. 285–287).

a. **The challenge to wives:**

1. Emerson's experience in receiving thousands of e-mails tells him that a wife vents when hurt and resentful. He writes: "Because she feels so vulnerable to her husband, who is typically strong and stubborn and quite possibly insensitive and unloving at times, she may color the facts a bit pink to solicit and gain sympathy" (p. 285). This even happens in women's prayer meetings and Bible studies as they "share their concerns." Women gain support by sharing with their girlfriends. How might a wife cross a line into slander?

   _____

   _____

   _____

   _____

2. As a wife, have you been guilty of crossing the line between sharing a concern and slandering your husband? Have your friends ever sided with your husband after your report?

_____

_____

_____

_____

3. Read the following verses and note the warning in each:

Proverbs 25:23: "The north wind brings forth rain, and a backbiting tongue, an angry countenance."

Proverbs 11:13: "Whoever goes about slandering reveals secrets, but he who is trustworthy in spirit keeps a thing covered" (ESV).

Ephesians 4:32: "Be kind and compassionate to one another, forgiving each other, just as in Christ God forgave you" (NIV).

4. Wives, what motivates you to forgive your husband, stay away from slander, and focus on his positive qualities?

_____

_____

_____

_____

b. **The challenge to husbands:**

Upon hearing of his wife's venting to her girlfriends, a husband can become infuriated by her one-sided report, and his anger can easily turn to bitterness and stonewalling.

1. Do you agree or disagree with Emerson's warning to husbands in the following quote?

"Realize, too, that [your wife] tends to turn to others for support. Yes, she can cross a line that you would not cross, but if you were a woman, you'd seek support, too, if your husband did not welcome you humbly and gently. Do not judge your wife as intending to embarrass you in front of others. That is not her goal. If you had been more tender with her, she would have come to you and not turned to others. She would have released her negative feelings as you empathized with her, listened to her burdens, and prayed with her. Remember, she is a goodwilled woman. Her aim is not to slander you but to connect with you! Forgive her!" (pp. 286–287).

2. Read the following scriptures and note the warning in each.

Colossians 3:19: "Husbands, love your wives and do not be embittered against them."

Proverbs 15:1: "A gentle answer turns away wrath, but a harsh word stirs up anger" (NIV).

Proverbs 15:18: "A hot-tempered man stirs up dissension, but a patient man calms a quarrel" (NIV).

Colossians 3:13: "Bear with each other and forgive whatever grievances you may have against one another. Forgive as the Lord forgave you" (NIV).

3. Husband, how much does your lack of empathy and anger stir up conflict in your marriage?

      A great deal   Somewhat   Not at all

4. Because of what you are learning about your wife's goodwill, how can you be less angry and more forgiving?

_____

_____

_____

_____

c. **Husbands and wives**: Will you commit to speaking Forgiving Words?

An unforgiving spirit is not compatible with the Jesus Way of Talking. Forgiving my mate is the way I learned Christ. Jesus forgave me, therefore I will forgive my spouse.

SESSION TWELVE

CHAPTER SIXTEEN: "THE JESUS WAY OF TALKING—PART III: TO LOVE OR RESPECT: BE THANKFUL, SCRIPTURAL— AND FAITHFUL"

In preparation for this session, read Chapter Sixteen, "The Jesus Way of Talking—Part III: To Love or Respect: Be Thankful, Scriptural—and Faithful."

In Session Eleven, we learned that the first three letters in T-U-F-T-S remind us to use Truthful, Uplifting, and Forgiving Words in order to follow the Jesus Way of Talking. We have two more strands of T-U-F-T-S to examine: Thankful Words and Scriptural Words.

T – THANKFUL WORDS: Since it is easy to be negative, focus on your mate's good qualities and express thanks with positive words of love or respect.

1. Paul describes Thankful Words as part of the Jesus Way of Talking (Ephesians 5:3–4). There he instructs the "giving of thanks" (v. 4). Jesus Himself put a high priority on thankfulness, and He expects His followers to give thanks to God and to others. When He healed ten lepers, He noted that only one of them—and a Samaritan at that!—returned to thank Him (Luke 17:11–19).

   a. How often do you thank your spouse for the things he or she does for you?

      Every day   1–3 times a week   Not much at all

   b. If you answered "not much at all," why do you withhold words of thanks?

      _____

      _____

      _____

      _____

c. When we focus on the negative, we lose sight of the positive. Though many things appear negative in your marriage, what happens if you thank your spouse for the positive? (Refer to pages 292–97 for insights.) Give an example from your marriage when you acted on this principle, and what happened as a result.

_____

_____

_____

_____

Unfitting Talk

2. In Ephesians 5:3–4 Paul warns us against obvious pitfalls such as immorality, impurity, and greed. He then adds "there must be no filthiness and silly talk, or coarse jesting, which are not fitting, but rather giving of thanks."

a. Why do you think Paul instructs the giving of thanks to counter filthiness, silly talk, and coarse jesting?

_____

_____

_____

_____

b. Long term, what do these unfitting remarks (filthy words, silly words, and coarse words) do to the spirit of a wife or husband? What do they do to you?

For example, what happens to a wife when a husband continually says such things as, "Oink, oink, Miss Piggy! Your second piece of cake I see!"? What happens to a husband when a wife does such things as roll her eyes, shake her head, and say, "You're such a jerk. You just don't get it!"?

_____

_____

_____

_____

c.   How have you stopped unfitting words designed to change your spouse, and focused on giving thanks for the positive qualities of your spouse?

_____

_____

_____

_____

d.   Do you think Thankful Words contradict Truthful Words? Explain.

_____

_____

_____

_____

Jesus Gives Thanks for Your Spouse

3. Jesus does not talk about us in the heavenly places with filthy words, silly talk, or coarse jesting.

a.   What happens in the heart of Christ when He hears us talk about our spouse in a way that He does not?

_____

_____

_____

_____

b.   Imagine Jesus giving thanks for your spouse to the Father. What do you hear Him saying? Write down several things. Does this help you voice the same to your spouse? Note: Because we are to give thanks when praying (Philippians 4:6; Colossians 4:2), Jesus would also (Romans 8:34).

_____

_____

_____

_____

Think to Thank

4. One needs to give thought to give thanks.

    a.   Husbands and wives too often keep a negative mental list of the things they would like their spouse to change. Fixating on the negative prohibits thanksgiving. Take the time to write five to ten positive things about your spouse (include those from question 3b). Keep this list handy for those times when you tend to focus on the negative. Offer thanks to the Lord AND to your spouse for at least one of these traits a day over the next several weeks and watch what happens.

_____

_____

_____

    b.   True or False: To convey words of love and respect to a spouse one must include Thankful Words.

_____

Rejecting the Thanks

5. Some spouses do not appear to receive words of thanks. They rarely acknowledge expressions of gratitude.

    a.   Why might a person not respond to words of thanks and even counter with, "You don't mean it"?

_____

_____

_____

_____

    b.   Does your spouse reject your sincere thanks? If so, should you stop? Why continue to give thanks?

_____

_____

_____

_____

c. Do you receive thanks? If not, how do you feel about quenching your spouse who gives thanks in obedience to God? Will you respond more positively in the days ahead?

_____

_____

_____

_____

The Thankful Person

6. You may find it unthinkable to give thanks when your marriage is difficult. But God calls you to give thanks to Him regardless of what happens in your marriage. You can pray, "God, I thank You for using this difficult time for a deeper purpose. I trust You, Lord."

a. 1 Thessalonians 5:18 says, "In everything give thanks; for this is God's will for you in Christ Jesus." Write a sentence in your own words expressing how you might give thanks even in the midst of the trials in your marriage.

_____

_____

_____

_____

b. Read the examples of testimonies of husbands and wives who learned to give thanks (pages 292–96) including Emerson's wife, Sarah. Which of these examples spoke to you the most? Write down two or three ideas that challenge and inspire you to apply thankfulness in your situation.

_____

_____

_____

_____

c. Have you considered that your lack of thanks toward your spouse evidences your lack of thanks toward God (1 Thessalonians 5:18)? Explain your thoughts.

_____

_____

_____

_____

Thanksgiving Is a Sacrifice

7. Psalm 50:23 says, "He who offers a sacrifice of thanksgiving honors Me."

a. Why do you think the psalmist used the word *sacrifice* to describe thanksgiving? What does it mean to sacrifice? (Read Sarah's story on pages 295–96 for insight.)

_____

_____

_____

_____

b. Before we move on to the next letter in T-U-F-T-S, make this commitment:

With God's help I will counter negative thoughts about my spouse by giving thanks for all his or her good qualities. I know Jesus does not let my weaknesses or faults control His view of me. He does not view me as worthless or make me the butt of silly jokes. I will treat my spouse as Jesus treats me. This is the way I learned Christ!

S - SCRIPTURAL WORDS: To stay the course in speaking words of love or respect, keep your heart in Scripture, trusting in and talking about His promises to help you.

Jesus and Scripture

8. Scriptural Words, the "S" in our acronym T-U-F-T-S, shows the Jesus Way of Talking, and helps us to stay on the Rewarded Cycle. Jesus models how to use Scriptural Words. He talked about the Scriptures and often asked His listeners, "Have you not read?" In Matthew 19:4–5 the Pharisees try to trap Jesus with questions about divorce. Jesus said, "Have you not read that He who created them from the beginning made them male and female and the two shall become one flesh?" Jesus always returned to God's truth.

a. Look up other examples of "Have you not read?"(Mark 2:25; 12:10, 26). How does it affect you when you read the phrase, "Have you not read?" What does this tell you about Jesus' view of Scripture?

_____

_____

_____

_____

b. During the temptations of Jesus, what did He say to Satan three times (Matthew 4:4, 7, 10)? Why do you think He said this?

_____

_____

_____

_____

c. If the Ephesians had "learned Christ" at all (see Ephesians 4:20), they understood how much importance He placed on the Scriptures. Do you view Scripture as Jesus viewed Scripture? Explain your view.

_____

_____

_____

_____

The Word of Christ

9. Colossians 3:16 says, "Let the word of Christ richly dwell within you."

a. What does Colossians 3:16 mean to you?

_____

_____

_____

_____

b.   Do you try to "let the word of Christ dwell within you"? How?

_____

_____

_____

_____

Again, No Magic Formula!

10. Speaking Scripture may or may not help the marriage.

a.   State briefly if you agree or disagree with the following statements, and why.

1.   The scriptural way of talking reveals the depth of my relationship to Jesus Christ.

_____

_____

_____

2.   To speak Scriptural Words, I must first ask, "Does the Bible say anything about this issue?"

_____

_____

_____

3.   Because I take seriously the Jesus Way of Talking, I will avoid saying anything that contradicts His words.

_____

_____

_____

4.   When I speak biblically my spouse may not respond. Not everyone responded positively to Jesus.

_____

_____

_____

b. How often during the day do you ask, "What would Jesus *say* (WWJS) at this moment in order to speak with love or respect?"

_____

_____

c. True or False?

1. When talking the scriptural way, I must always try to quote some Bible verse to my spouse.

_____

2. If I speak Scripture into my marriage, I will get most everything I want from my spouse.

_____

Speaking Scripture to Each Other

11. Depending on God's Word draws couples together, especially during times of adversity.

a. Emerson received the following excerpt from a young husband: "Our relationship is improving because we're trying to follow Christ's example. We're trying to lay down our lives for one another and regard each other as the more important one. Within the last year we have grown spiritually beyond anything we ever expected. God is doing this work in our lives and we are truly amazed. The ability of God to change our hearts and to change habits that we've established over five years of marriage (and even twenty-seven years of life) is more amazing to me than any sign or wonder I've ever seen or heard of" (p. 302).

Did you see the two Bible verses this husband paraphrased (1 John 3:16; Philippians 2:3)? What did this couple specifically do that the Bible told them to do? How did these scriptures help them?

_____

_____

_____

_____

b. As a couple, are you "speaking to one another in psalms and hymns and spiritual songs" (Ephesians 5:19)? How might you encourage each other to share

Scripture? (For example, Sarah sometimes quotes a line from a song, like Don Moen's lyric, "God will make a way, Where there seems to be no way.")

_____

_____

_____

_____

c. Do you allow your spouse to share helpful scripture, or do you ridicule him/her?

_____

_____

_____

_____

d. As Satan misused scriptures during the temptation of Jesus, doing so for self-serving purposes, husbands and wives can be guilty of clubbing a spouse with scripture for self-serving purposes. What does God think of a person who is not "accurately handling the word of truth" (2 Timothy 2:15)?

_____

_____

_____

_____

e. The Bible also teaches that there are times when it is wise to remain quiet instead of quoting a Bible verse (James 1:19, 26; 1 Peter 3:1–2). In what ways have you seen scripture inappropriately spoken?

_____

_____

_____

_____

Praying Based on Scripture

12. Jesus said, "Ask, and it will be given to you. . . . For everyone who asks receives. . . . Or what man is there among you who, when his son asks for a loaf, will give him a stone? Or if he asks for a fish, he will not give him a snake, will he? If you then, being evil, know how to give good gifts to your children, how much more will your Father who is in heaven give what is good to those who ask Him!" (Matthew 7:7–11).

a. How can you apply these verses to your marriage? Have you placed your confidence in the words of Jesus and the Bible to guide you in what to ask?

_____

_____

_____

_____

b. Jesus said, "Again I say to you, that if two of you agree on earth about anything that they may ask, it shall be done for them by My Father who is in heaven" (Matthew 18:19). James says, "You do not have because you do not ask" (James 4:2). Why might God, according to these two verses, not work in some marriages?

_____

_____

_____

_____

c. Emerson shares that the e-mails he receives reveal that many couples who believe in the Bible do not pray together. If you and your spouse do not pray together regularly, what prevents you?

_____

_____

_____

_____

d. Does asking God mean you can ask for anything and God will give it? Read what James had to say about that, and paraphrase in your own words. "You ask and do not receive, because you ask with wrong motives, so that you may spend it on your pleasures" (James 4:3).

_____

_____

_____

_____

e. When you pray together based on the Scriptures, does this qualify for speaking scripturally to one another?

_____

_____

_____

_____

Initiating Husbands and Responsive Wives

13. As a husband and wife team, you can start praying together using the promises in Scripture as the basis of your prayers. Look in the back of your Bible. Often the publishers provide a list of favorite promises.

    a. Husband, rate your leadership in this area of prayer:

      Pretty good   Mediocre   Not so good

    b. Wife, how would you respond if your husband led in prayer?

      Positive   Unresponsive   Critical

    c. Agree or Disagree? When a wife sees her husband's dependency on Jesus, she more readily depends on her husband's leadership.

      _____

Seven for Heaven

14. Praying together seven minutes a day starts you on a path to praying as a couple. Remember, if you refuse to "ask" God, you deprive yourself of untold blessings since "you do not have because you do not ask" (James 4:2).

    a. As a husband, if you and your wife do not pray together, will you start a seven-minute time each day (I call it "Seven for Heaven!") in which you thank God and ask God to fulfill certain biblical promises?

      _____

b. As a wife, what might you do, respectfully, to encourage praying with your husband for seven minutes a day?

_____

_____

_____

_____

c. Keeping in mind the discussion on pink and blue differences, is it okay for you and your spouse to pray differently?

_____

_____

Remember, prayer does not serve as a platform to send a message to your spouse that they need to change!

The Commitment

15. Get excited about talking the Jesus Way! Not only can you talk with Scriptural Words, you can apply T-U-F-T-S to your everyday speech.

a. To avoid the pitfall of neglecting Scripture, make the following commitment in prayer: *"Lord, keep my heart focused on the Scriptures and trusting Your promises to help me always speak words of unconditional love or respect."* Do you have any hesitations about making this commitment? If so, what are they?

_____

_____

_____

_____

b. Unconditional love and respect tests one's faith in Christ and the Scriptures. Those grasping this truth stay the course, certain to hear God's "Well done!" Do you grasp and envision this?

_____

_____

c. In our discussion of the Rewarded Cycle, we studied the Jesus Way of Talking with Truthful, Uplifting, Forgiving, Thankful, and Scriptural Words. But the key is one word—*unconditional.* At the end of the day, you can measure how well you have lived according to Love and Respect by looking back and evaluating your words. Did you speak in unconditional ways? This is a high standard, too high to achieve in human strength alone. For this reason, the Rewarded Cycle stresses the need to do everything in your marriage as unto God. Your faithfulness—to God, to His Word, and to your spouse—brings you through. One husband shares his struggle to stay on the Rewarded Cycle after years of experiencing the Crazy Cycle. Read his powerful testimony of faithfulness in "An Unconditional Love Story" on pages 304–308. How does this story speak to you?

_____

_____

_____

_____

In God Always Trust

16. In the conclusion, Emerson encourages his son, Jonathan, and daughter-in-law, Sarah, to trust God.

   a. Read this chapter. What spoke to you the most and why?

   _____

   _____

   _____

   _____

   b. Your marriage is a tool and a test to deepen and demonstrate your love and reverence, and your trust and obedience, toward Jesus Christ. What practical difference does this truth make in your life?

   _____

   _____

   _____

   _____

c. Will God reward you for your trust and obedience even if your spouse never talks to you in meaningful ways? But, when you talk in loving or respectful ways, if your spouse has goodwill, do you believe you have effectively cracked the communication code between you?

_____

_____

_____

_____

As a Result of This Study

17. Will you make the following commitment?

With God's help, I will use words of unconditional love and respect. I realize I will not do this perfectly, but I intend to move in this direction. I agree to act on the following:

I will speak lovingly or respectfully regardless of how my spouse acts or speaks. Yes

_____

I will speak lovingly or respectfully because I want to reverence and obey God. Yes

_____

When I fail to speak words of unconditional love or respect perfectly, I will ask for forgiveness—first from God and then from my spouse—and I will keep trying. Yes _____

CHA-CHING!

APPENDIX I

Suggestions for Group Leaders Using *The Language of Love & Respect Workbook* in a Group Setting

Before using this workbook with your small group . . .

1. Read "Before You Begin Your Study of *The Language of Love & Respect*" (p. vi).

2. Complete several sessions of the workbook to become thoroughly acquainted with its design and function. You should always be a session or two ahead of the group to provide adequate time to internalize the material and decide which questions to emphasize with your group. If possible, have your spouse study along with you and use the discussion ideas for couples throughout the workbook.

3. Check your leadership style. Facilitating a group study of a book like *The Language of Love & Respect* is a great responsibility. The spouses in your group represent marriages in different circumstances and stages, some strong, others weak. As you lead your group, seek to be:

Relaxed and casual, but organized and able to keep things moving. Let people share, give opinions, and even disagree a bit, but don't be afraid to sum things up and move to the next question or topic.

Caring and sensitive, always trying to be aware of what others might be thinking or feeling at the moment. Some couples in your group will probably see a lot of humor in certain questions and be quite able to enjoy what is going on. Others could be hurting and unhappy, not finding the proceedings to be as much fun. You may spot couples or perhaps individuals you need to contact outside the group, to guide them in their study, pray with them, or possibly refer them to someone who can give help that you cannot.

Accepting and nonthreatening. For example, if someone comes up with an opinion that is totally counter to what Emerson sometimes refers to as "typical" or "generally speaking," do not be defensive or argumentative. Let everyone give opinions, then sum up by saying, "According to Emerson's extensive experience and research on marital communication, this is what he finds to be the norm or what is typical of men and women, husbands and wives. He knows there are exceptions to any 'general rule,' but he has also found that regardless of how people think or act, they all need Love and Respect in communication."

Experienced and empathetic. Ideally, you and your spouse have studied the workbook together, and you have learned how to slow and stop the Crazy Cycle. You know what it takes to keep the Energizing Cycle humming. And you know and readily admit that at times you need wisdom and humility that you can only get from the Rewarded Cycle. Your enthusiasm and transparency as you share your communication problems and what you have learned will do much to get the group to relax and open up. (You don't have to have a perfect marriage to qualify to lead a small group through the workbook. Ideally, however, if you and your spouse are leading the group together, it would be beneficial for you to be in agreement about communicating the Love and Respect way!)

Willing to use tough love and respect in regard to everyone doing the homework. As a rule, any couple willing to join a study of *The Language of Love & Respect* should be highly motivated to put in the necessary time to improve their communication. If you are holding meetings once a week, suggest that couples will need to invest a minimum of one hour weekly to the workbook. As they get into their study, they may soon be spending much more than that.

Remind everyone: "Your study of *The Language of Love & Respect* should be top priority because your marital communication is top priority. Your assignments in *The Language of Love & Respect Workbook* are 'home work' done for the sake of your marriage and your home. This study has to do with improving (even saving) your marriage. It deserves your best effort because your marriage deserves your best effort."

Dependent on God's leading. Prayer must be a major part of your preparation for every meeting. And while leading a meeting, silently pray: "Lord, help us all right now; give me the right words to say, or prompt another member of our group to share something that can help someone else." If you get a question you can't answer, admit it and say you will try to find an answer by the next meeting. Throughout the week, pray for each of your group members, and for each marriage represented. Contact your group members during the week to see how they are doing. If a couple is on the Crazy Cycle, offer to pray with them over the phone. Never be pushy, but always be available and interested.

4. Plan your meetings and what you want to cover. As you have probably already seen, there is a lot of material in this workbook. The twelve sessions are organized around the flow of material in *The Language of Love & Respect*, as you move from the Crazy Cycle to the Energizing Cycle and finally the Rewarded Cycle. Some sessions cover one chapter of *The Language of Love & Respect*; others cover more. Obviously many sessions contain far more material than you can cover in one meeting. You will want to pick and choose questions that you believe will meet the needs of your group.

Also important is how much time you have for each meeting. You should plan on one hour minimum, but ninety minutes or two hours would be better, particularly as people get involved in discussing their problems and sharing insights they have gleaned from reading *The Language of Love & Respect*. As you divide the material to develop meeting plans, keep these points in mind:

- Go through a session and decide how much of it you will use for a meeting.
- Choose questions that cover the key truths of a given chapter in *The Language of Love & Respect*. All of the material is interesting, but keep in mind your goal for the meeting—the essential points you want to make.
- Go over all the questions you think you might use and analyze each one for how suitable it is for "public group consumption." Some of the questions asked in this workbook are sensitive; the answers people write will be, in some cases, things they want to keep private. Some questions are probably best avoided altogether; others could be used if you do some checking with your group members and also give some introductory explanations. Always stress that no one has to talk or share what is written in his or her workbook.
- If you would like more help with planning meetings and/or to move through the material more quickly, contact http://loveandrespect.com/CodeLight/ and ask for "Meeting Plans for Your Small Group."

APPENDIX II

"GIVE ME SOMETHING NEW AND DIFFERENT!"

I heard an unforgettable story. When the leader of a small-group Bible study announced "Ephesians" as the focus of the study, a young man who several months earlier had come to Christ said, "Oh, let's look at something else. I already read the book of Ephesians."

I laughed. He was announcing, "Give me something new and different. Having read Ephesians, I marked that off my reading list." Ephesians to him was a mere short story, and re-reading short stories was a waste of his time.

We chalk his comments up to immaturity. Several years later, deeper in his walk with Christ, he'll echo Paul: "Oh, the depth of the riches both of the wisdom and knowledge of God! How unsearchable are His judgments and unfathomable His ways!" (Romans 11:33). Recognizing the unfathomable wisdom of Ephesians, he may request from his group leader, "Might we study Ephesians again, and then again?" Perhaps this young man will have the attitude of Dr. Merril Tenney, one of the greatest New Testament professors to live. Dr. Tenney, who received his Ph.D. from Harvard, exclaimed in his class that I took on the Gospel of John, "I have taught the Gospel of John over one hundred times, yet each time I learn so much more." That comment blew me away. Even a genius like Dr. Tenney knew that he could not tap the depth of God's wisdom. For example, what you and I read today, whether the Gospel of John or the Book of Ephesians, will speak to us more deeply tomorrow as we humble ourselves before these ancient truths. In other words, keep reading the same thing, over and over, and watch what happens to your soul!

I find it intriguing that Peter wrote his last epistle as a reminder. He conveyed to his audience that earlier a body of ideas from God descended from heaven and nothing extra had emanated. So, he pens, "I consider it right, as long as I am in this earthly dwelling, to stir you up by way of reminder" (2 Peter 1:13). He also writes, "This is now, beloved, the second letter I am writing to you in which I am stirring up your sincere mind by way of reminder, that you should remember the words spoken beforehand by the holy prophets and the commandment of the Lord and Savior spoken by your apostles"

(2 Peter 3:1–2). Peter challenges the believers to seize the divine reality that there is only so much truth revealed to the church through the prophets, apostles, and Jesus. We read in Jude 1:3 that "the faith . . . was once for all delivered to the saints" (ESV). Tomorrow your Bible will not have new teachings added. Truth starts in Genesis and stops in Revelation.

Interestingly, Paul preached this whole body of truth in three years in Asia. We read, "For I did not shrink from declaring to you the whole counsel of God. . . . Therefore be alert, remembering that for three years I did not cease night or day to admonish everyone with tears" (Acts 20:27, 31 ESV). I recall a pastor, who studied the Bible thirty hours a week for his pulpit ministry, exclaiming that after a decade of studying and preaching the Bible verse by verse, that he realized there were no new principles. Though thousands of Hebrew and Greek words can be read, a limited number of concepts and principles exist. He found himself revisiting synonymous ideas. This is why Systematic Theology is a course of study. God gave us a system of truth!

How does all of this apply to a workbook on marriage? Don't expect God to keep giving you a new and different revelation on marriage! In the first century AD, God said about marriage what He intended to say. The revelation on marriage "was once for all handed down to the saints." Given you learned the foundational truths on marriage, God's "reminders" suffice. For example, the pinnacle truth of a husband loving his wife remains constant for the church. Colossians 3:19 and Ephesians 5:33 remain unchanged. Nothing new or different descends from God's throne to replace these sacred texts to husbands. Mature husbands only need reminders and practical examples to apply love more regularly and deeply.

Friends, when doing this study, don't look for new truths but for new ways to apply the truths you know. When you do, thrilling things happen. For example, in the book *The Language of Love & Respect*, on which this workbook is based, the biblical outline on marriage stays the same as in my first book, *Love and Respect*. I cannot find new foundational truths in the Bible on marriage. For instance, the concepts of C-O-U-P-L-E (Closeness, Openness, Understanding, Peacemaking, Loyalty, and Esteem) stay rooted in the salient scriptural passages to husbands. (This is a systematic theology on marriage.) God forbids me to exceed what is written in Scripture on these divine truths (1 Corinthians 4:6). Though *The Language of Love & Respect* goes deeper into the hundreds of new ways to apply love and respect to the mouth, providing fresh testimonies and recent research to help you in your applications, this workbook does not present never-before-seen biblical truths! I echo Peter. I write this workbook "by way of reminder" (2 Peter 1:13).

I hope this excites you. I hope you don't say, "Oh, I already read Ephesians 5:33 about husbands loving and wives respecting. Give me something new and different!" As you study this workbook, I hope you say, "Lord, there is always something I can learn more deeply about love and respect in marriage. Teach me, Lord."